Elegant Meals

ELEGANT MEALS

Savina Roggero
Wines suggested by Antonio Piccinardi

CRESCENT BOOKS
NEW YORK

Picture sources:
Ai Kidosaki: pps 130-131, 142-143; Fusako Holthaus: pps 74-75, 128-129; Jun Hida: pps 22-23, 92-93; Kazuyuki Sakai: pps 12-13, 52-53; Kenichi Fujimoto: pps 158-159; Maki Irie: pps 32-33, 42-43, 82-83; Masako Hamano: pps 30-31, 146-147; Nobu Kawakami: pps 26-27, 44-45, 76-77, 134-135; Mario Rossi: pps 8-9, 10-11, 18-19, 28-29, 38-39, 50-51, 54-55, 64-65, 78-79, 84-85, 88-89, 96-97, 102-103, 112-113, 114-115, 122-123, 144-145, 150-151, 152-153, 174; Shōko Murakami: pps 166-167; Studio Adna: pps 20-21, 34-35, 48-49, 56-57, 58-59, 60-61, 62-63, 68-69, 70-72, 86-87, 98-99, 100-101, 104-105, 106-107, 108-109, 110-111, 116-118, 120-121, 138-139, 162-163, 168-169, 170-171, 172-173; Tadahiko Ogawa: pps 14-15, 16-17, 24-25, 46-47, 66-67, 94-95, 140-141, 148-149; Tatashi Tatsuoka: pps 124-125, 126-137, 132-133, 136-137, 154-155, 160-161; Tomiyasu Hasegawa: pps 36-37, 40-41, 80-81, 90-91.

Translated by Sara Harris
Copyright © 1981 Shogakukan Publishing Co., Ltd., Tokyo – for the illustrations
Copyright © 1984 Arnoldo Mondadori Editore S.p.A. Milano – for the international edition
Copyright © 1984 Arnoldo Mondadori Editore S.p.A. Milano – for the Italian edition
Copyright © 1985 Arnoldo Mondadori Editore S.p.A. Milano – for the English translation

Published 1985 by Crescent Books, distributed by Crown Publishers, Inc.

Library of Congress Cataloging in Publication Data

Roggero, Savina.
  Elegant meals.

  Translation of: I grandi piatti.
  1. Entertaining. 2. Cookery. I. Title.
TX731.R5513 1985   641.5   85–12763
ISBN 0–517–48051–4

h g f e d c b a

Printed and bound in Italy by Arnoldo Mondadori Editore, Verona

Contents

Meat

Veal and mushrooms Istanbul

Preparation and cooking time: 1 hour

Serves 4: 1¾ lb veal escalopes, thinly sliced from the leg
● ⅓ cup oil ● juice of ½ lemon ● 1 large onion ● ¾ cup dry white wine ● ½ pint light stock ● 3 cups mushrooms ● 1 tablespoon tomato paste ● 1 oz bacon ● scant ½ cup cream ● paprika ● salt ● pepper ● cornstarch (optional)

Serve with pilaf rice (see recipe, p. 176) using 1¼ cups long grain rice

Suggested wines

Merlot del Collio, Nuits-Saint-Georges, Beaujolais Villages

Suggested menu

Penne with radicchio
▷ Veal and mushrooms Istanbul
Caramelized pears

1 Clean the mushrooms and place in a bowl of water mixed with the lemon juice to prevent them from discoloring. Dry and slice just before sautéing.

2 Chop the onion and the bacon; sauté in a saucepan in 2 tablespoons oil. As soon as the onion starts to turn brown, add the sliced mushrooms. Stir and fry gently over moderate heat for about 10 minutes. Season with a pinch of salt and a little freshly ground pepper. Remove from heat.

3 Pound the veal slices with a meat mallet dipped in cold water; trim off any fat and cut into strips.

4 Dust the strips of veal with flour, place in a sieve and shake to get rid of excess flour.

5 Sauté the strips in the remaining oil over fairly high heat; turn so that they color evenly and sprinkle with a pinch of salt. Using a slotted spoon, transfer the veal strips to a heated dish, cover and keep warm.

6 Stir the wine into the juices in the pan stirring with a wooden spoon until the wine has almost completely evaporated.

7 Stir in the tablespoon of tomato paste and the light stock (preferably veal stock); then dribble in the cream while stirring.

8 Add the sautéed vegetables and bacon to the sauce, then the veal strips. Stir until every strip of veal is coated with sauce and sprinkle with a generous pinch of paprika. Cook for 10–15 minutes until the sauce has reduced slightly. Thicken with a little cornstarch dissolved in cold water if desired. Serve with pilaf rice.

Classic veal fricassee

Preparation and cooking time: About 2 hours

Serves 4: 2¼ lb veal cut into small cubes (use boned breast, short ribs, shoulder or stewing pieces) ● 3½ pints light stock (made with 1 lb chicken and 1 lb veal trimmings, bones, etc) ● 1 small carrot, 1 leek and 1 onion stuck with a clove ● a bouquet garni (a few stalks of parsley, thyme and a bay leaf) ● ¼ lb skinned baby onions ● 5 oz mushrooms (preferably ceps, dried and presoaked if fresh are not available) ● generous ¼ cup butter ● ½ cup flour ● 3 egg yolks ● generous ½ cup cream ● juice of ¼ lemon ● a little grated nutmeg ● 1 tablespoon finely chopped parsley ● salt ● pepper

Suggested wines

Marqués de Riscal, Chianti, Bordeaux rouge

Suggested menu

Mushroom and tomato pasta
▷ Classic veal fricassee
Apricot and kirsch soufflé

1 Place the cubed veal in a large saucepan and pour in enough strained stock to cover veal by at least ¾ in. Bring to a gentle boil and continue cooking while skimming off the scum from the top.

2 Add the carrot, leek, onion and bouquet garni and continue to simmer gently for 1 hour 50 minutes.

3 Cook the onions separately for about 40 minutes, adding 2 tablespoons butter, 3 tablespoons water and a pinch of salt so that they are lightly glazed when done.

4 Clean, trim and thinly slice the mushrooms and boil for about 10 minutes in a generous ½ cup water.

5 Strain the veal and reserve the cooking stock; place the veal in another saucepan and add the onions and strained mushrooms; keep warm.

6 Melt the remaining butter, stir in the flour and then gradually stir in the hot stock from the veal.

7 Cook the sauce over low heat for 15 minutes, stirring with a wooden spoon and removing any scum that collects during cooking. Beat the egg yolks with the cream and a few drops of lemon juice; dribble this into the veal stock sauce, stirring continuously and briskly so that the egg mixture will not curdle. Add a pinch of nutmeg and bring almost to a boil.

8 Pour the sauce through a sieve onto the veal, onions and mushrooms and stir the veal in the sauce over a low heat; remove from heat as soon as it starts to boil and transfer to a deep warm serving dish. Sprinkle with parsley and serve.

Veal crêpes Roquefort with carrot purée

Preparation and cooking time: 1 hour 30 minutes

Serves 4: 4 5-oz veal loin chops ● 2 tablespoons butter ● generous cup dry white wine ● salt ● pepper

For the crêpes: 2 eggs separated ● 1 cup flour ● 1 pint milk ● butter ● salt

For the sauce: 2 tablespoons butter ● 2 oz Roquefort cheese ● 3 tablespoons brandy ● scant cup cream ● salt ● pepper

For the carrot purée: 6 carrots ● 2 medium-sized potatoes ● 6 tablespoons cream ● 2 tablespoons butter ● salt ● pepper

Garnish: 4 whole shelled walnuts ● 16 hazelnuts ● 4 almonds

Suggested wines

Cabernet di Pramaggiore, Richebourg, Romanée Saint-Vivant

Suggested menu

Black olive canapés
▷ Veal crêpes Roquefort with carrot purée
Cinnamon pear soufflés

1 To make the crêpes, work the egg yolks into the flour, whisk in the milk, beat egg whites until stiff and add to mixture with a pinch of salt. Heat a little butter in a small omelette pan and pour in enough batter to cover bottom. When lightly browned on one side, turn and continue cooking on the other side. Repeat until all the batter has been used up.

2 Soften butter and blend with cheese and brandy to make a thick sauce.

3 Dice and boil carrots and potatoes, then purée. Keep warm in a double boiler, stirring in the butter, cream and a pinch of salt and pepper.

4 Sauté the veal chops briskly in 2 tablespoons hot butter, season with a little salt and pepper, add the white wine and continue cooking until it has evaporated. Take up the meat and slice crosswise.

5 Work the cheese sauce into the remaining butter and juices in the pan; simmer briefly over moderate heat.

6 Add the sliced veal to the sauce and cook gently for a minute or two to allow the meat to moisten and absorb the flavor.

7 Spread out a crêpe, place a few pieces of veal in the center, season with freshly ground pepper and fold the crêpe.

8 Repeat with all the crêpes, then pour a little sauce on each and serve with a few spoonfuls of purée, using a fork or knife to shape elegantly. Decorate each crêpe with a walnut, an almond and a few hazelnuts.

Carpetbag steaks

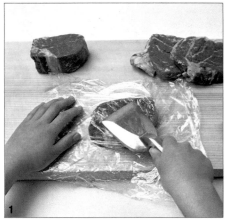

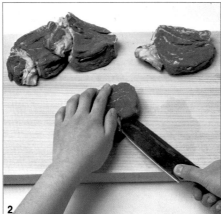

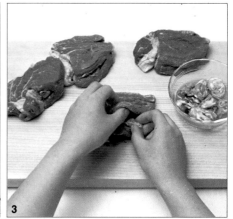

Preparation and cooking time: 1 hour

Serves 4: 4 thick club, sirloin or porterhouse steaks •
2 tablespoons butter • 16 fresh oysters • salt • pepper

For the sauce: 2 finely chopped shallots • 4 ripe
tomatoes • 1 pint stock made with a stock cube •
½ cup port • 3 tablespoons butter • 1 oz *beurre manié*
(3 tablespoons flour worked into 1 tablespoon butter –
slightly softened, not melted) • salt • pepper

Suggested wines

Brunello di Montalcino, Saint-Emilion,
Chambertin

Suggested menu

Cream of asparagus soup with chervil and ham
▷ Carpetbag steaks
Blancmange

1 Cover the steaks with
plastic wrap and pound
with a meat mallet.

2 Make an incision in one
side of each steak.

3 Push two oysters into
each steak and secure
with a toothpick.

4 *To prepare the sauce*:
Melt the butter in a
saucepan, add the shallots
and sauté until golden
brown.

5 Pour in the port and
cook until it has almost
completely evaporated.

6 Add the peeled, seeded

and roughly chopped
tomatoes, the remaining
oysters, also chopped,
and the stock; season. Let
the sauce simmer and
reduce before adding the
beurre manié, stirring the
mixture as the butter
melts and releases the
flour into the sauce to
thicken it. While the sauce
is reducing fry the steaks
in the very hot butter,
seasoning them. Make
sure the steaks and their
contents are warmed
through without
overcooking. Transfer the
steaks to a hot serving
dish and pour the sauce
over each one.

15

Roast tenderloin of beef with wine sauce

Preparation and cooking time: 1 hour 10 minutes

Serves 4: 2¼ lb beef tenderloin ● 1½ pints stock made with a stock cube ● ½ lb cubed lean beef ● 1 onion ● 1 carrot ● 1 celery stalk ● 1 teaspoon tomato paste ● ¾ cup dry white wine ● scant ½ cup cornstarch ● ⅔ cup oil ● salt ● pepper

Garnish: watercress

Suggested wines

Château Lafite Rothschild, Barbaresco, Reserva Especial 1922

Suggested menu

Cream of lettuce soup
▷ Roast tenderloin of beef with wine sauce
Lemon chiffon

16

1 If not already done, tie the meat with string so that it will hold its shape while cooking.

2 Sprinkle generously with salt and freshly ground pepper.

3 Heat 6 tablespoons oil in a heavy sauté pan or skillet over a fairly high flame and add the beef; cook for 15 minutes to seal flavor and brown evenly all over. Remove the meat from the oil.

4 Wrap the beef in foil and then wrap in a towel. Keep warm (this way the meat will not dry out or toughen).

5 Trim, wash and prepare the vegetables. Chop the onion coarsely, dice the carrot and celery; sauté in the remaining 6 tablespoons of oil.

6 Transfer the vegetables to a second sauté pan or heavy-bottomed casserole, add the cubed beef; stir and sauté for a few minutes before seasoning with salt and pepper. Add the wine and when this has almost completely evaporated, sprinkle in the cornstarch.

7 Stir in the tomato paste mixed with the hot stock; simmer over moderate heat for 40 minutes, skimming off any scum from the surface.

8 Strain off the cooking liquid into a saucepan; blend the diced beef and the vegetables in a food processor. Pour this mixture back into the cooking liquid and bring to a boil. Remove the wrappings and string from the tenderloin, cut into fairly thick slices and garnish with watercress. Serve the sauce very hot, passing it around separately.

Argentine braised beef

Preparation and cooking time: 2 hours 50 minutes

Serves 6: 3 lb rump roast, cut into 1-in cubes ●
generous $\frac{1}{4}$ cup shortening ● $\frac{1}{3}$ cup oil ● 2 large onions
● 2 bell peppers ● 5 large ripe tomatoes ● 1 celery
stalk ● 3 medium-sized potatoes ● 10 oz pumpkin (skin
and seeds removed) ● 2 small apples ● 2 cups cooked
sweet corn (fresh or canned) ● 5 oz grapes ● a
bouquet garni (1 bay leaf, 1 tablespoon chopped
marjoram, 1 tablespoon thyme, 1 tablespoon chopped
parsley) ● $1\frac{1}{4}$ cups dry white wine ● $1\frac{1}{2}$ cups stock ●
generous cup rice ● 3 peppercorns ● 1 clove garlic ●
salt ● cayenne pepper

Suggested wines

Saint-Emilion, Barsac, Inferno

Suggested menu

Pumpkin soup
▷ Argentine braised beef
Orange cream

1 Brown the beef in the melted, very hot shortening in a large, heavy-bottomed casserole or enamel pot.

2 Sauté the sliced onions, the crushed clove of garlic and the peppers (seeds and pith removed and coarsely chopped) in the oil over gentle heat, using an earthenware or cast iron pot or skillet. Add the chopped tomatoes.

3 When the vegetables have cooked through, transfer them with their juices to the casserole containing the meat. While stirring, add the chopped celery and the bouquet garni. Season with salt, cayenne pepper and the peppercorns.

4 Add the white wine a little at a time. When this is considerably reduced, pour in the hot broth or stock and stir. Cover and cook over low heat for 1 hour 15 minutes stirring at frequent intervals.

5 While the beef and vegetables are simmering, peel and dice the potatoes, apples and pumpkin. Stir into the meat and vegetable mixture when it has cooked for the length of time given above. Continue cooking for a further 30 minutes.

6 Stir in the cooked, drained sweet corn.

7 While the beef is braising cook the rice in plenty of salted boiling water; when it is tender but not mushy drain and then stir into the beef together with the grapes. Adjust the seasoning and cook for a few minutes longer. Serve immediately in a large, heated earthenware dish or, for a better effect, in a large pumpkin.

This dish is spectacular when served in a pumpkin. Prepare the pumpkin by slicing off the top, scooping out all the seeds and washing the inside; heat for 15 minutes in a hot oven. Alternatively, serve in a rustic-looking deep earthenware dish.

19

Marinated roast beef

Preparation and cooking time: 2 hours 50 minutes + 2 days for marinating the beef (*see instructions opposite*)

Serves 4: 2¼ lb rib eye or rump roast ● ⅓ cup oil ● a few tablespoons all-purpose flour ● 1 medium-sized onion ● 1 carrot ● 1 celery stalk ● 1 clove garlic ● pinch of freshly grated fresh ginger ● 1 small container yoghurt ● salt ● pepper

For the marinade: 1 onion ● 2 shallots ● 1 carrot ● 2 cups dry red wine ● 6 tablespoons red wine vinegar ● 1 cup water ● 1 bay leaf ● a few cumin seeds ● thyme ● salt ● 5 peppercorns

Suggested wines

Colli orientali Cabernet, Pinot noir, Bordeaux rouge

Suggested menu

Spaghetti with tuna and leek sauce
▷ Marinated roast beef
Chocolate bananas

1 Prepare the marinade following instructions below right. Immerse beef in the cooled marinade. Cover and leave in the refrigerator for two days, turning the beef several times.

2 After two days, take the beef out of the marinade and dry with paper towels. Set marinade aside. Season a few tablespoons of flour with salt and freshly ground pepper and flour the meat. Heat the oil in a large, heavy-bottomed fireproof casserole or enamel pot and brown the beef all over; when well colored, remove from pot and set aside.

3 In the same pot, sauté the finely sliced onion, carrot, celery and chopped garlic very gently for 5 minutes, stirring frequently.

4 Return the beef to the pot, pour the reserved marinade over it, add the grated fresh ginger and bring slowly to a boil.

5 As soon as the marinade starts to boil, turn down the heat, cover and simmer very slowly for 2½ hours; use two wooden spatulas or tongs to turn the beef frequently so that it cooks evenly; whisk a tablespoon of yogurt into the cooking liquid whenever the meat is turned.

6 When the beef is done, take out and allow to cool to room temperature. Strain the cooking liquid through a fine sieve, return to the pot and reheat.

7 Slice the cooled meat, place in the strained sauce and allow to heat over a very low flame. Arrange the slices on a heated serving platter, cover with a little of the sauce and pass around the rest of the sauce separately.

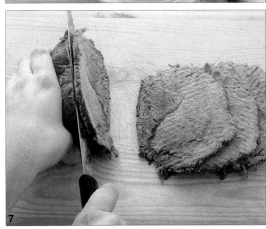

To prepare the marinade: Wash, peel and finely slice the onion, shallots and carrot and place in a large enamel or stainless steel casserole or pot with the other ingredients. Bring to a gentle boil, stirring from time to time; lower the heat and simmer gently for 10 minutes. Leave to cool to room temperature.

Chicken liver and egg loaf

Preparation and cooking time: 1 hour 40 minutes

Serves 6: $2\frac{1}{4}$ lb finely chopped or ground lean beef •
2 large onions, finely chopped or minced • scant $\frac{1}{2}$ cup
freshly grated Parmesan cheese • 2 eggs • 10–11 oz
diced and cooked mixed vegetables or frozen mixed
vegetables, such as carrots, peas, potatoes, etc. •
6 chicken livers • scant 2 tablespoons butter • 2
hard-boiled eggs • scant $\frac{1}{4}$ cup brandy • 1 cup fresh
tomato sauce or sieved fresh or canned tomatoes •
6 tablespoons oil • salt • pepper

Garnish: watercress • sliced tomatoes

Suggested wines

Médoc, Bianco di Custoza, Chablis

Suggested menu

Mushroom and ham rice timbale
▷ Chicken liver and egg loaf
Melon filled with fruit salad

1 Sauté the finely chopped or minced onions gently in the oil, until pale golden brown.

2 Place the chopped or ground beef in a bowl, add the raw eggs, the sautéed onion, the mixed vegetables and the grated Parmesan cheese; season with a little salt and freshly ground pepper. Work all the ingredients together using a fork until the mixture is well blended and smooth.

3 Heat the butter in a skillet and fry the trimmed, washed and dried chicken livers briskly; season with salt and pepper, add the brandy and continue cooking until it has completely evaporated or until the livers are cooked.

4 On a piece of foil on the work surface, shape a third of the beef mixture in a rectangle, leveling the surface with the hand.

5 Make two shallow, parallel depressions lengthwise in the surface of the meat; fill these with the quartered hard-boiled eggs and half the chopped cooked chicken livers.

6 Cover with another third of the meat mixture, make two more lengthwise cuts in the loaf and fill with the remaining chopped chicken livers. Cover with the rest of the meat mixture.

7 Wrap the foil around the loaf and press to give an even shape.

8 Remove the foil; place the meat loaf on a lightly oiled cookie sheet. Cook for 30 minutes in a preheated oven at 400°F, then turn down the heat to 350°F and cook for another 30 minutes. Garnish with watercress and serve with fresh tomato sauce.

Beef olives

Preparation and cooking time: 1 hour 50 minutes

Serves 4: 8 fairly thin pieces of beef (such as flank steak, cut against the grain or rump roast cut into cross-grained slices, each trimmed to measure about 8 in × 8 in ● 1 large onion ● 2 carrots ● 1 celery stalk ● 4 large ripe tomatoes ● 1 pint tomato juice ● scant cup red wine ● 3 tablespoons oil ● 3 tablespoons butter ● 1 oz *beurre manié* ● 3 tablespoons milk ● salt ● pepper
For the stuffing: 1 generous cup lean ground pork ● 1 generous cup finely chopped or ground lean beef ● pinch of thyme ● pinch of powdered bay leaf ● a few ground fennel seeds ● pinch of ground coriander ● salt ● pepper

Suggested wines

Juliénas, Chianti Putto, Beaujolais Villages

Suggested menu

Rice with anchovies and herbs
▷ Beef olives
Chocolate bananas

1 Cover the slices of beef with plastic wrap and beat gently with a meat mallet.

2 Prepare the filling: place the ground pork and beef in a bowl and add the seasonings and herbs; mix well until all the ingredients have combined in a smooth paste.

3 Place two flattened pieces of beef so that they slightly overlap, place a quarter of the stuffing in the middle and roll up, tying firmly with string.

4 Heat 2 tablespoons butter in a skillet with the oil. When it is very hot add the beef "olives"; brown on all sides. Season with salt and pepper, remove from pan and keep warm.

5 Clean and trim the carrots and celery and peel the onion before chopping into small pieces. Melt the remaining butter in a large saucepan, add the vegetables and sweat gently over low heat.

6 Add the beef "olives," pour in the wine and as soon as it has evaporated, add the peeled, seeded and diced tomatoes and the tomato juice; stir and then leave to simmer gently for about 30 minutes. Remove the beef "olives" from the pan and keep hot on a heated serving platter.

7 Add the milk to the sauce and beat in with a whisk or hand-held beater.

8 Add the *beurre manié*. Season with a little salt and freshly ground pepper. Push the sauce through a sieve (or blend in an electric blender or food processor) and pour over the beef "olives," some of which can be sliced and ready to serve.

New England boiled beef and chicken

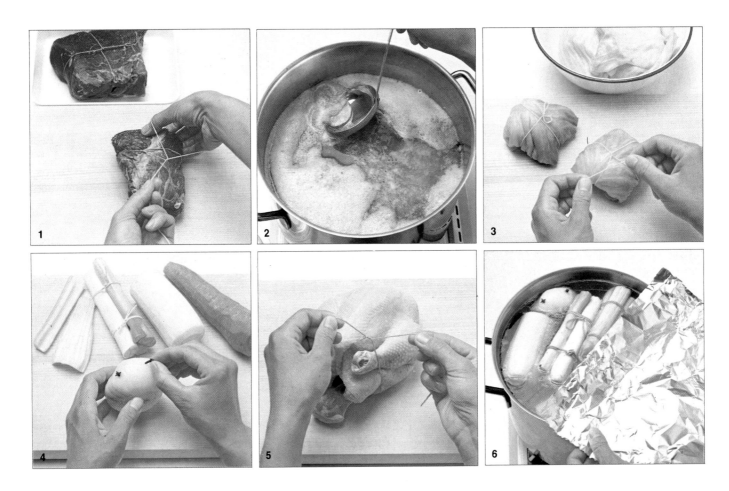

Preparation and cooking time: 2 hours 30 minutes

Serves 8: 2¼ lb top round steak ● 1¾ lb rump roast ●
2¼ lb chicken ● 1 small cabbage ● 1 onion ● 1 leek ●
2 carrots ● 2 celery stalks ● 1 clove garlic ● 1 turnip ●
2 cloves ● salt

Suggested wines

Barolo, Chambertin, Saint-Emilion

Suggested menu

Penne with radicchio
▷ New England boiled beef and chicken
Banana almond crunch

1 Tie the two cuts of beef together firmly with string.

2 Place the meat in a large pot with 3 quarts plus 1 pint water and a generous pinch of coarse salt; bring to a boil. Use a ladle to skim off the scum on the surface. Lower the heat and simmer over a very low flame for at least 1 hour.

3 Wash the cabbage; remove the hard stalk and strip off the leaves. Place the leaves in groups of four, one on top of the other; roll up each pile and tie with string.

4 Wash the leek, cut in half lengthwise and tie at top and bottom. Peel the turnip and the onion; stud the onion with the two

cloves. Scrape the carrots, wash the celery stalks and cut into 3–4 in lengths.

5 Wash and dry the chicken and truss with string.

6 Add the vegetables and chicken to the pot containing the beef, cover with foil or a tight-fitting lid and bring to a boil.

Lower heat and simmer for 1 hour 15 minutes. Remove strings from chicken and vegetables. Serve each person with a selection of carved meats and some of the vegetables.

Jamaican loin of pork

Preparation and cooking time: 1 hour 30 minutes

Serves 4: 2¼ lb boneless loin of pork ● ½ cup oil ●
2 onions ● 2 cloves garlic ● 4 large ripe tomatoes ● a
bouquet garni (a few sprigs parsley, 1 bay leaf, a few
sprigs of thyme) ● 1 cinnamon stick ● ¾ cup dry white
wine ● generous pinch grated nutmeg ● few drops
Tabasco sauce ● salt ● pepper

Garnish: sautéed bananas

Suggested wines

Lander Selección, Moulin-à-vent, Chianti

Suggested menu

Special sweet corn soup
▷ Jamaican loin of pork
Apple meringue

1 Tie the boned loin of pork securely so that it will keep its shape as it cooks; sprinkle with a little salt and freshly ground pepper; brown well on each side in the oil in a large, heavy-bottomed casserole or enamel pot.

2 When the pork is golden brown all over, transfer to a stainless steel plate, cover and place over a saucepan of boiling water to keep the meat warm.

3 Sauté the finely chopped onions in the oil used to brown the meat; fry very gently until transparent but do not brown; place the loin of pork on top of the onions, sprinkle with the finely chopped garlic. Blanch and peel the tomatoes, cut in quarters and remove the seeds; add to the pork. Sprinkle the grated nutmeg into the casserole and crumble in the cinnamon stick; add the bouquet garni and 2 or 3 drops of Tabasco sauce.

4 Season with a little more salt and freshly ground pepper, pour in the dry white wine, cover and bring to a gentle boil over fairly low heat. Place in a preheated oven at 400°F for 1 hour, basting frequently.

5 Remove the pork from the casserole, leaving it at room temperature to cool. Pour the cooking liquid through a fine sieve.

6 When the pork has cooled, remove the string and carve into slices. Pour a little of the strained juices into a shallow serving dish, arrange the pork slices in the dish, slightly overlapping one another, and cover with the remaining strained juices. Cover with foil and return to the oven for 10–15 minutes at 350°F.

The original Jamaican recipe calls for a garnish of sliced bananas sautéed in butter and seasoned with salt and pepper, which adds a further dimension to the flavor and gives the dish a more authentic, exotic touch.

Roast pork with prune filling

Preparation and cooking time: 1 hour 40 minutes

Serves 4: 1¾ lb boneless shoulder of pork • 4 spareribs of pork • 1 carrot • 1 onion • 1 stock cube • ½ cup oil • ¾ cup red wine • 1 tablespoon pearl barley • 1 tablespoon melted butter • 1 teaspoon soy sauce • 1 tablespoon all-purpose flour • salt • pepper

For the filling: 20 dried prunes, soaked for 30 minutes in warm water, drained and then left to stand for 1 hour in red wine.

Garnish: watercress

Suggested wines

Chambertin, Brunello di Montalcino, Château Latour

Suggested menu

Cream of leek and potato soup
▷ Roast pork with prune stuffing
Coffee ice cream charlotte

1 Unroll the shoulder roast and trim to form a rectangle.

2 Drain the prunes and reserve the wine. Pit the prunes and arrange 10 of them at one end of the rectangle of pork. Sprinkle with a little salt and freshly ground pepper and roll up the meat so that the prunes end up in the middle. Tie the roll with string.

3 Pour 6 tablespoons of oil into a roasting pan, place the meat in the pan and sprinkle with salt and freshly ground pepper; arrange the spareribs, the coarsely chopped onion and carrot around the rolled pork and brush the meat with the remaining oil. Place in a preheated oven (400°F) and roast for 35 minutes, turning the pork frequently and basting with the juices.

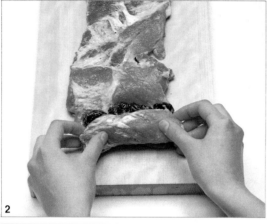

4 When the pork is crisp and well browned, take up and set aside. Place the roasting pan over a low heat and pour in the reserved heated wine into which the stock cube has been crumbled. Stir well.

5 Mix barley, 1 tablespoon melted butter, 1 teaspoon soy sauce and 1 tablespoon flour. Add this mixture to the sauce and stir until it thickens.

6 Strain the sauce through a metal sieve into a saucepan.

7 Add the remaining soaked prunes to the sauce, cook for 20 minutes over a gentle heat. When the meat has cooled, remove the string and slice. Arrange in a shallow, ovenproof dish, together with some of the sauce, cover with foil and heat in the oven. Serve with the prunes and garnish with watercress. Serve the remaining sauce in a sauceboat.

Medallions of pork

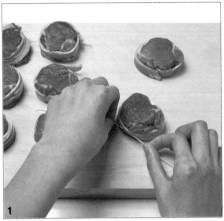

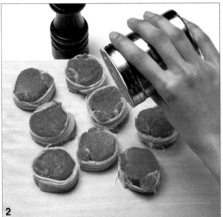

If a thicker sauce is preferred, add a *beurre manié* (made with 1 tablespoon butter and 1 teaspoon flour) 15 minutes before the pork is done and stir constantly with a wooden spoon. Mashed or puréed potatoes go very well with this dish.

Preparation and cooking time: 45 minutes

Serves 4: 8 1 in-thick medallion steaks cut from a pork tenderloin • 8 thin slices of bacon • 2 shallots • 8 black olives • 1 celery stalk • 3 tablespoons Cognac • 1 cup stock • 1 cup dry red wine • 3 sieved raw ripe tomatoes • 2 tablespoons butter • 2 tablespoons oil • salt • pepper

Garnish: black olives (pitted)

Serve with baby carrots, boiled asparagus and baked zucchini

Suggested wines

Pommard, Chianti, Médoc

Suggested menu

Pumpkin soup
▷ Medallions of pork
Pears Cardinal

1 Wrap a piece of bacon around each piece of pork and secure well with a string.

2 Season with salt and freshly ground pepper.

3 Chop the shallots and celery finely and sauté gently in a large skillet in the oil and butter.

4 Place the pork medallions in the skillet and brown lightly on both sides. Add the Cognac; flame and shake the pan gently until the flames have died down; remove the pork from the pan and keep warm.

5 Stir the sieved tomatoes into the cooking juices left in the pan; add the red wine and stock and simmer gently for 15 minutes. Return the medallions to the pan and simmer for 30 minutes. Cover, but allow enough steam to escape so the liquid will gradually reduce. Remove the string from each medallion and transfer to a heated serving dish. Pour the cooking juices over the medallions and garnish each with a black olive. Surround with the selection of vegetables.

Stuffed zampone with lentils

Preparation and cooking time: 3 hours 30 minutes (+ 5 hours' soaking time)

Serves 4: 1 2–2¼ lb cured pig's trotter (*zampone*) ● 1 lb lentils (lentils must be pre-soaked for 2 hours in cold water) ● scant ¼ cup bacon fat ● 1 cup full-bodied red wine ● 3 tablespoons tomato paste ● scant 1½ cups light stock ● 2 tablespoons butter ● 1 tablespoon all-purpose flour ● 1 onion ● salt ● pepper

Suggested wines

Sangiovese, Oltrepò Pavese rosso, Saint-Emilion

Suggested menu

Beef consommé
▷ Stuffed zampone with lentils
Fresh fruit mosaic

1 Soak the pig's trotter in a large bowl of cold water for 5 hours.

2 Puncture the skin of the trotter at intervals with the prongs of a carving fork; wrap the trotter in a clean cloth and place in a pot full of fresh cold water; simmer very gently for 3 hours. While it is cooking, prepare the lentils (step 3). After 3 hours, turn off the heat and leave the trotter in the cooking liquid for another 30 minutes to cool slightly.

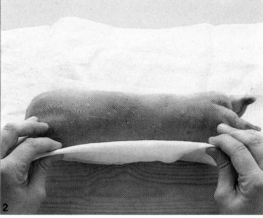

3 Sauté the chopped onion in the fat and butter, add the drained lentils and season with a little salt and freshly ground pepper.

4 Add a tablespoon of flour and pour in the red wine, stirring constantly.

5 Mix the tomato paste with the hot stock and add to the lentils.

6 Bring to a boil and cook for 2½ hours, stirring now and then and adding more stock whenever necessary. Adjust the seasoning, adding more salt to taste. Serve the trotter very hot, carved into slices and surrounded by the lentils.

In Italy this dish is served at Christmas and is the traditional fare for celebrating New Year's Eve because it is supposed to bring luck for the coming year. It is important to cook the trotter very slowly for a long time until the meat is tender and gelatinous. It is ready when the prongs of the carving fork slide in easily. Pre-prepared pigs' trotters or *zamponi* are available in Italian shops and delicatessens and these only need warming through for 10 minutes in boiling water – saving a great deal of time and effort.

Pork chops in Dijon mustard sauce

Preparation and cooking time: 1 hour

Serves 4: 12 pork chops ● 6 tablespoons oil ● ¾ cup dry white wine ● ¾ pint cream ● 2 onions ● 2 tablespoons butter ● 6 tablespoons gravy made with half a stock cube dissolved with 1 tablespoon butter into 1½ tablespoons dry white wine ● 5–6 tablespoons Dijon mustard ● salt ● pepper

Suggested wines

Marzemino, Margaux, Médoc

Suggested menu

Asparagus and rice mold
▷ Pork chops in Dijon mustard sauce
Orange frost

1 Trim off the fat from the pork chops with a very sharp knife.

2 Melt the butter in a skillet, add the chopped onions and sauté until a pale golden brown.

3 Heat the oil in another skillet and when very hot add the lightly floured pork chops. Brown on both sides and then season with a little salt and freshly ground pepper. Pour in the cream and finish cooking the pork chops over a gentle heat; when they are done, remove them from the sauce and keep warm on a heated serving plate.

4 Stir the sautéed onions into the sauce.

5 Stir in the mustard.

6 Add the stock, butter and wine mixture and reduce over a moderate heat; pour the sauce over the pork, sprinkle with chopped parsley and serve.

Ham en croûte

Preparation and cooking time: 1 hour 5 minutes (+ thawing time for the frozen pastry)

Serves 4: A 2¼ lb smoked ham • 14 oz frozen puff pastry • 1 egg • 1 tablespoon powdered mustard • 3 tablespoons Marsala (sweet dessert wine) • 1 tablespoon butter • pepper

Suggested wines

Juliénas, Valpolicella, Rosé de Touraine

Suggested menu

Cream of lettuce soup
▷ Ham en croûte
Apricot and kirsch soufflé

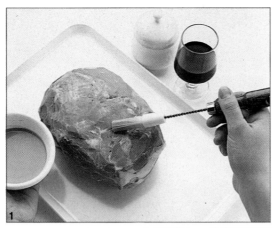

1 Leave the pastry to thaw for several hours at room temperature. Mix the mustard in a small bowl with the Marsala, add a little freshly ground pepper and mix well until the mixture is smooth. Trim off any fat from the ham and brush with the mustard.

2 Roll out the puff pastry into a fairly thin sheet, large enough to envelope the ham without stretching. Reserve a few small pieces for decoration.

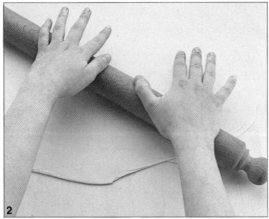

3 Place the ham in the center of the sheet of pastry and fold the pastry over the meat, pinching the two edges together. Seal both ends the same way.

4 Cut decorations out of the remaining pastry to cover the join, brushing the underside of each piece with a little water or milk if necessary to make it stay in place.

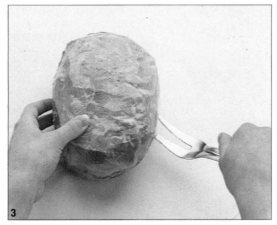

5 Beat the egg with a pinch of salt in a small bowl. Prick the surface of the pastry case in a few places to allow steam to escape while cooking. Brush the pastry with the egg glaze.

6 Preheat the oven for 15 minutes to 400°F. Grease a cookie sheet with butter, cover with a double layer of foil and grease the top surface of the foil with butter; place the ham carefully on the foil and cook until the pastry is golden brown all over. Remove from oven, transfer to a heated serving platter and serve at once while piping hot.

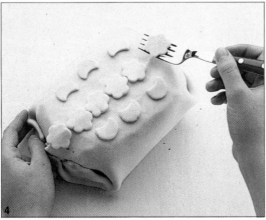

This is a very impressive dish to serve and delicious to eat. The original version comes from Baden, Germany, near the French border. It calls for a case of bread dough rather than the easier puff pastry, and at one time the local people would take their ham en croûte to the baker for cooking. The puff pastry case makes a more elegant dish and lends a more delicate and appetizing taste to the ham.

Sweet-and-sour pork chops with figs

Preparation and cooking time: 1 hour

Serves 4: 12 small pork chops ● 6 tablespoons oil ●
$\frac{3}{4}$ cup dry white wine ● 2 gherkins ● 2 finely chopped
shallots ● 6 tablespoons gravy (made with half a stock
cube dissolved with 1 tablespoon butter into
1 tablespoon white wine) ● 4 canned figs (drained,
syrup reserved) ● juice of $\frac{1}{2}$ lemon ● $\frac{1}{2}$ tablespoon
tarragon ● 1 teaspoon of syrup from the canned figs ●
$\frac{1}{2}$ cup cream ● 1 tablespoon chopped parsley ● 1
tablespoon all-purpose flour ● generous $\frac{1}{4}$ cup butter ●
salt ● pepper

Suggested wines

Barbaresco, Châteauneuf-du-Pape, Pura Sangre

Suggested menu

Hot savory toasts
▷ Sweet-and-sour pork chops
Blancmange

1 Season the pork chops with a little salt and freshly ground pepper.

2 Heat the oil in a large skillet and fry the pork on both sides; pour in the dry white wine and continue cooking until the wine has completely evaporated; remove the pork chops from the skillet and keep warm.

3 Melt the butter in the skillet, stir in the flour with a wooden spoon, making sure there are no lumps.

4 Add the cream, the stock, butter and wine mixture and the finely chopped gherkins and shallots.

5 Continue stirring and add the figs and the teaspoon of syrup.

6 Sprinkle the chopped tarragon and the lemon juice into the sauce and simmer for a few minutes over moderate heat to allow the sauce to reduce and thicken. Arrange the pork chops on a heated serving plate or directly onto the dinner plates, cover with sauce and sprinkle with the finely chopped parsley.

The contrast between the sharp taste of the gherkins and the bland cream complements the sweetness of the figs and gives this dish a very unusual sweet-and-sour flavor.

Terrine of pork

Preparation and cooking time: 1 hour

Serves 4: $1\frac{1}{3}$ cups chopped pork • 1 boneless chicken breast, diced • $\frac{1}{4}$ cup shredded bacon • 1 large onion • 2 cloves garlic • 1 bay leaf • $\frac{3}{4}$ cup dry white wine • scant $\frac{3}{4}$ cup stock made with a stock cube • 2 tablespoons butter • a few sprigs parsley (flat-leaved, if available) • 1 pitted black olive • pinch of paprika • salt • pepper

Suggested wines

Port, Marsala, sherry

Suggested menu

▷ Terrine of pork
Chicken Madagascar
Apples flamed in rum

1 Peel the onion and chop finely.

2 Shred the bacon, using a very sharp knife.

3 Melt the butter and add the onion, the finely chopped garlic and the bay leaf and sauté gently.

4 Add the shredded bacon and the chopped pork and sauté briskly over a higher heat. Add a generous pinch of paprika. Pour in the wine and cook until it has completely evaporated.

5 Add the stock and the diced breast of chicken and leave to simmer over moderate heat until the meat is cooked through.

6 Allow the mixture to cool a little before placing in the electric blender or food processor; blend until the mixture is smooth.

7 Transfer the mixture to a bowl, season with salt and pepper and stir well.

8 Place the bowl in the refrigerator and chill for a few hours. Just before serving transfer to an earthenware dish or terrine, press down firmly and make a ribbed pattern on the surface with the prongs of a fork. Place a black olive in the center and surround it with a few parsley leaves.

Pork with orange sauce

Preparation and cooking time: 2 hours 10 minutes

Serves 4: 1¾ lb loin of pork • 2 carrots • scant ½ cup brandy • 3 large juicy oranges • ½ cup dry white wine • ¼ cup potato flour or 4 tablespoons cornstarch • a few peppercorns • 1 bay leaf • 2 tablespoons butter • generous ½ cup milk • salt • pepper

Suggested wines

Zinfandel Napa Valley, Collio Cabernet, Margaux

Suggested menu

Vegetable and cheese quiche
▷ Pork with orange sauce
Apple and amaretto zabaglione

44

1 Tie up the loin of pork with string so that it will keep its shape.

2 Wash and scrape the carrots, and slice into rounds. Heat the butter in a pot and when it has just melted stir in the carrots and sauté for a few minutes. Add the meat and brown on all sides. Season with a little salt and freshly ground pepper; sprinkle with the brandy and when it has evaporated, pour in the dry white wine.

3 Crumble the bay leaf over the meat, add 2 pints water and cover.

4 Cook over a low heat for about 1½ hours, spooning the juices over the pork every now and then and removing any scum.

5 Use a cannelling knife to cut thin strips of peel from the three oranges and blanch in ½ pint water for 2 minutes.

6 Strain the orange liquid through a sieve.

7 Take up the pork, remove the string and keep warm on a hot serving dish. Strain the cooking juices into a small saucepan and stir in the potato flour (or cornstarch) dissolved in ½ cup milk, add the orange-flavored liquid and heat over a moderate flame, stirring until the mixture thickens. Remove the membrane from the orange segments and add these to the sauce together with the blanched strips of peel. Pour the sauce over the pork and serve.

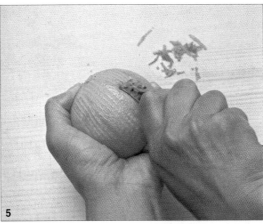

Pork chops in lemon sauce

Preparation and cooking time: 1 hour 20 minutes

Serves 4: 8 pork chops • ¼ cup butter • salt • pepper

For the sauce: 2 lemons • 1 pint stock • ¾ cup dry white wine • 1 tablespoon tomato paste • *beurre manié* (made with 1 tablespoon butter and 1 teaspoon flour) • scant 2 tablespoons butter • salt • pepper

Garnish: watercress

Serve with potato, carrot and pea purées (*see recipes*, pp. 175–6)

Suggested wines

Costa Blanca, Pommard, Juliénas

Suggested menu

Hot mozzarella hors-d'oeuvre
▷ Pork chops in lemon sauce
Pineapple rings in rum custard

1 Remove the zest of the lemons and cut into julienne strips; reserve the peeled lemons.

2 Place the julienne strips in a pan, cover with cold water, blanch for 2 minutes, then drain.

3 Heat the butter in a skillet and fry the pork chops until they color on both sides; season. When the pork is cooked through, take up and keep warm.

4 *To prepare the sauce*: Add the wine and the stock to the cooking juices and heat until it has considerably reduced.

5 Stir in the tomato paste, remove from heat and mix in the *beurre manié*; return to the heat and stir constantly.

6 Add the strips of lemon peel and the whole lemon segments (pith and membrane removed). Season. Simmer gently for 15 minutes. Pour the sauce over the pork chops on the serving dish or individual plates. Serve with creamed potatoes, puréed carrots and a purée of peas (piped decoratively using a fluted nozzle and a piping bag); garnish with sprigs of watercress.

Crown roast pork

Preparation and cooking time: 2 hours 30 minutes

Serves 6: 9 pork spareribs, uncut

Stuffing: ½ cup finely chopped or minced cooked ham ●
scant ½ cup finely chopped or minced pork ● 1 cup
fresh soft breadcrumbs soaked in ½ cup milk and
squeezed out ● 3 tablespoons freshly grated Parmesan
cheese ● 1 egg ● 1 tablespoon Dijon mustard ● a few
drops Worcestershire sauce ● small bunch parsley,
finely chopped ● oil ● ½ cup stock ● salt ● pepper

Garnish: small round tomatoes, parsley

Suggested wines

Brunello di Montalcino, Côte-Rôtie, Taurasi

Suggested menu

Cream of lettuce soup
▷ Crown roast pork
Pears, figs and almonds in honey sauce

1 Trim the ends of the spareribs by cutting away about 1½ in of meat from between the ribs and making small slits between the bones at the meaty end so that the rack can be bent around (smooth, bonier side outwards) to form a crown.

2 Tie up the crown roast and place in a roasting pan greased with oil.

3 *To prepare the stuffing*: Mix together the chopped ham, pork, egg, parsley and the grated Parmesan cheese.

4 Add the fresh fine breadcrumbs, the mustard, the Worcestershire sauce, a pinch of salt and a little freshly ground pepper. Mix thoroughly with a wooden spoon until well blended and smooth.

5 Spoon the stuffing into the center of the crown roast.

6 Cover the crown loosely with foil and cook in a hot oven (400°F) for 1½ hours. After about 20 minutes pour ½ cup of hot stock into the roasting pan and baste the meat at frequent intervals with the combined juices and stock from the bottom of the pan. When the roast pork is ready to serve, place a small paper crown over each trimmed bone. Garnish with tomatoes and parsley.

Turkish lamb with rice pilaf

Preparation and cooking time: About 2 hours (+ 2½ hours for soaking the rice)

Serves 6: 2½ lb leg of lamb, cut into cubes ● pinch of cinnamon ● ¾ cup butter ● 1 lb rice ● 2 pints boiling stock made with stock cubes ● 1 finely chopped onion ● ⅓ cup pine nuts ● 1 oz seedless white raisins (soaked) ● 6 large ripe skinned tomatoes (canned tomatoes may be used) ● ½ lb lamb's liver ● 1 tablespoon finely chopped parsley ● pinch of sugar ● salt ● pepper

Suggested wines

Rosé de Touraine, Rosé de Provence, Grignolino

Suggested menu

Bresaola rolls with ricotta stuffing
▷ Turkish lamb and rice pilaf
Rainbow salad
Pears Bellevue

1 Wash the rice in a sieve under cold water; transfer to a bowl and cover with hot water; leave to stand for 2½ hours.

2 Sauté the lamb in a skillet for 15 minutes in scant ½ cup butter, until the pieces have browned evenly. Season with salt and transfer to an ovenproof casserole; place in a preheated oven (350°F) for 1½ hours, moistening occasionally with a few spoonfuls of hot stock.

3 Sauté the chopped onion in ¼ cup butter in a saucepan. Add the drained white raisins and the pine nuts and continue cooking for a few minutes.

4 Crush the tomatoes with a fork. Add to the saucepan; pour in all the stock except for 1 scant cup and season with salt, pepper, a pinch of sugar and cinnamon.

5 Simmer for a few minutes and then add the soaked drained rice, cover tightly and place in the oven, still at 350°F and cook until the rice is *al dente*.

6 While rice is cooking, sauté the trimmed, washed and chopped liver in 3 tablespoons butter, add a pinch of salt and when the rice is done, mix in the liver and parsley. Spoon the rice pilaf into the center of a heated serving platter, arrange the cooked lamb around it and serve at once.

Lamb Provençal

Preparation and cooking time: 1 hour

Serves 4: 1½ lb boned lamb chops (or 14 noisettes) ●
2 zucchini ● 2 eggplants ● 2 large but not overripe
tomatoes ● generous pinch mixed dried herbs ●
1½ cups oil ● salt ● pepper

For the tomato sauce: 12 large ripe tomatoes ● ½ onion
● 1 clove garlic ● 5 tablespoons olive oil ● salt ●
pepper

Suggested wines

Valpolicella, Rosé de Touraine, Castillo de Tiebas

Suggested menu

Bosun's noodles
▷ Lamb Provençal
Cherry charlotte

1 If the butcher has not already done so for you, bone the lamb, and slice into thick medallions. Flatten with a meat mallet.

2 Peel lengthwise strips from the zucchini, slice in rounds and fry in half of the oil, preheated until very hot; take up with a slotted spoon and drain on paper towels. Prepare the eggplant in the same way.

3 Heat the remaining oil in the same saucepan and sauté the lamb until well browned on both sides; season with a pinch of salt and freshly ground pepper; take up and set aside on a warm plate.

4 *To prepare the tomato sauce*: Trim, wash and dry the tomatoes; remove the seeds and chop coarsely. Cook slowly in a saucepan with half an onion and a clove of garlic for about 30 minutes. Allow the sauce to reduce and thicken. Pass through a sieve or liquidizer and add a little salt, pepper and olive oil.

5 Grease an oval ovenproof dish with oil and spoon in about ½ cup of the tomato sauce.

6 Arrange the fried vegetables, meat and 2 raw sliced tomatoes in rows across the ovenproof dish, beginning with a row of fried zucchini then raw tomatoes, followed by fried eggplant and the sautéed lamb. Repeat until all the ingredients have been used up. Sprinkle with the dried herbs.

7 Top with the remaining tomato sauce and bake in a fairly hot oven (350°F) for 20 minutes. Serve immediately.

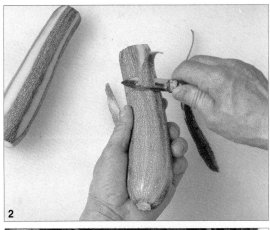

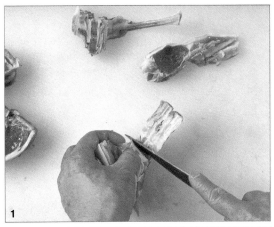

Spanish roast lamb

Preparation and cooking time: 1 hour 30 minutes

Serves 4: A 3–3¼ lb shoulder of baby or milk-fed lamb
● 4 cloves garlic ● ½ cup melted fresh pork fat ● 1 lb
new potatoes ● several sprigs of rosemary ● salt ●
pepper

Suggested wines

Cabernet di Pramaggiore, Nuits-Saint-Georges,
Santa Maddalena

Suggested menu

Pumpkin soup
▷ Spanish roast lamb
Exotic fruit salad

1 Peel and crush 3 cloves of garlic and rub into the surface of the lamb or insert into slits in the meat so that it is well-flavored.

2 Sprinkle salt and freshly ground pepper on each side of the shoulder before putting it onto a rotisserie spit. Roast in a preheated oven for 40 minutes or until tender at 525°F; place a roasting pan under the lamb to catch the juices and fat as it cooks.

3 At frequent intervals dip a glazing brush into the fat that collects in the roasting pan and baste the shoulder. Once the lamb has started to brown evenly all over, baste every 5–10 minutes, dipping the brush into the melted fresh pork fat. When the lamb is cooked (a rosy pink inside unless you prefer it well done), remove carefully from spit and wrap in foil to keep warm. Turn oven heat down to 350°F.

4 Scrub off the skin of the new potatoes and toss in a large bowl with the chopped rosemary, a crushed clove of garlic and coarse salt.

5 Place the potatoes and rosemary in the hot fat left in the roasting pan, and roast for 30 minutes with the oven at 350°F. Turn the potatoes at least once during cooking so that they are evenly coated with fat.

6 When the potatoes are golden brown, unwrap the lamb and place in the pan; leave in the oven for a few minutes. Serve the lamb on a very hot platter, garnished with a few sprigs of fresh rosemary.

This delicious way of presenting lamb, typical of traditional Spanish provincial cooking, is both simple to prepare and very nourishing. If young lamb is difficult to find, use the shank half of a leg from the youngest, tenderest lamb available.

Jellied rabbit mold

Preparation and cooking time: 1 hour 50 minutes (+ chilling time)

Serves 4: A 3–3½ lb rabbit ● 2 pints gelatine (use 1½ packets of powdered gelatine dissolved in 1½ pints light meat stock, flavored with ¾ cup sherry, cooled but still liquid) ● 1 cup baby carrots, sliced into rounds ● 1 cup baby onions ● 1 cup small mushrooms ● ¼ cup pitted black olives ● ¼ cup pitted green olives ● 3 tablespoons capers ● ¼ cup butter ● 1 cup dry white wine ● 6 gherkins ● 3 tablespoons oil ● 3 tablespoons wine vinegar ● 1 clove ● 1 bay leaf ● 1 clove garlic ● 1 tablespoon chopped chervil ● salt ● pepper

Suggested wines

Pinot noir, Nebbiolo, Moulin-à-vent

Suggested menu

Cream of shrimp soup
▷ Jellied rabbit mold
Apricot and kirsch soufflé

1 If the butcher has not already done so for you, chop the rabbit into 7–8 pieces (do not use the head). Brown the rabbit in the butter and oil in a heavy-bottomed pot.

2 Season the rabbit pieces with salt and a little freshly ground pepper before adding the onions, sliced mushrooms, clove, bay leaf and garlic.

3 Cook for 15 minutes, then pour in the wine and vinegar. Cover and simmer over very low heat for 1 hour 20 minutes, turning and mixing occasionally with a wooden spatula.

4 *To prepare the savory jelly*: While the rabbit and vegetables are cooking, dissolve the gelatine in the hot broth; when it has dissolved stir in the sherry.

5 Rinse out a large mold with cold water and spoon in enough warm gelatine mixture to cover the bottom. Chill in the refrigerator.

6 When this first layer of jelly has set arrange the cooled pieces of rabbit in the mold, layering them with the slices of raw carrot, chervil, sliced mushrooms, onions and the drained, dried capers.

7 Pour a little gelatine into the mold, chill, and proceed with the next layer. When all the rabbit and vegetables have been set in the jelly, finish off with the remaining liquid gelatine and chill for at least 2 hours.

8 To serve the jellied rabbit, dip the mold almost up to its rim in a large bowl of hot water, cover with the serving plate and then turn the mold upside down on the plate. Garnish with gherkins and black and green olives.

Saddle of venison with juniper berries

Preparation and cooking time: 2 hours (+ 6 hours for the marinade)

Serves 8: A 4½ lb saddle of venison ● ½ cup oil ● a bouquet garni (sprigs of parsley and thyme and 1 bayleaf) ● 2 quarts stock made with a stock cube ● scant cup cream ● ¾ cup dry white wine ● 6 juniper berries ● ½ cup gin ● 1 onion ● 1 celery stalk ● 1 teaspoon tomato paste ● *beurre manié* (made with scant 1 tablespoon butter and 1 teaspoon flour) ● salt ● pepper

Serve with chestnut purée (see recipe, p. 175)

Suggested wines

Barbaresco, Châteauneuf-du-Pape, Chambertin

Suggested menu

Cream of leek and potato soup
▷ Saddle of venison with juniper berries
Apple and amaretto zabaglione

1 In a large bowl combine the oil, bouquet garni, juniper berries (lightly crushed with a meat mallet), onion, celery stalk cut in several pieces, salt and pepper. Cover and leave to marinate for 6 hours.

2 Cut the saddle of venison into cubes, place in a heavy, ovenproof casserole and brush with the oil from the marinade.

3 Sprinkle some freshly ground pepper on the venison, add the herbs and other solids from the marinade and place in a hot oven (400°F), moistening with the remaining oil mixed with 3–5 tablespoons of stock.

4 After about 20 minutes, sprinkle the meat with a little salt, turn and when browned, remove from oven. Sprinkle with the gin and flame.

5 When the flames have gone out, cover and continue cooking over very low heat; moisten occasionally with hot stock.

6 When the venison is tender, remove from the casserole and keep warm over boiling water.

7 Remove and discard the bouquet garni and the juniper berries and then push the vegetables and sauce through a sieve or *mouli-légumes*.

8 Add the *beurre manié* and the tomato paste to the sauce. Cook over low heat for a few minutes, stirring constantly until the sauce thickens; stir in the cream gradually, followed by the wine. Continue stirring until the sauce is smooth and creamy; remove from heat and pour over the venison. Serve with a chestnut purée.

Marinated beef with polenta

Preparation and cooking time: 3 hours (+ 4 hours for the marinade)

Serves 4: 2¼ lb beef for stew • ¼ cup butter • 5 tablespoons oil • 2 pints full-bodied red wine • 1 large onion stuck with a clove • 2 carrots • 2 celery stalks • bay leaf • a few sprigs of rosemary • a few sage leaves • 5 peppercorns • 1 clove garlic • thyme • 2 tablespoons flour • salt • pepper

Serve with slices of polenta or cornbread, piping hot from the oven

Suggested wines

Hermitage, Chianti classico, Barsac

Suggested menu

▷ Marinated beef with polenta
Pear and walnut cake

1 Wash, trim and chop the carrots and celery. Cut the meat into chunks. Place in a bowl and add the onion, bay leaf, sage, rosemary, sliced garlic, thyme, peppercorns and the red wine; cover and leave to marinate in a cool place for 4 hours, turning often.

2 Take up the pieces of meat, dry and sauté in a heavy saucepan or ovenproof earthenware pot in the oil and butter.

3 When the meat is well-browned all over, sprinkle with salt and then with the flour and pour in the marinade, including the vegetables and herbs.

4 Cover and simmer gently for 2½ hours, stirring frequently with a wooden spoon.

5 Take up the pieces of meat with a slotted spoon, and reserve. Push the vegetables through a fine sieve and return with the cooking juices to the pot with the meat.

6 Continue simmering the meat in the strained liquid for 10–15 minutes, until very tender; add a little more wine as needed. Serve with very hot slices of polenta.

Roast wild boar

Preparation and cooking time: 2 hours 30 minutes (+ 3 days for the marinade)

Serves 4: 2¼ lb haunch of wild boar • 1 pint full-bodied red wine • 5 tablespoons red wine vinegar • 1 bay leaf • 5 juniper berries • 1 onion • 1 carrot • 1 celery stalk • 2 crushed cloves of garlic • 3–4 sage leaves • ½ cup bacon, finely diced • 9 oz ceps (dried mushrooms, presoaked to soften and plump) • 1 teaspoon potato flour • ¼ cup butter • ½ cup cream • small cinnamon stick • 1 pint stock made with stock cube • salt • pepper

Serve with slices of baked polenta or cornbread

Suggested wines

Cabernet Sauvignon Napa Valley, Chianti, Margaux

Suggested menu

Ham, egg and cheese risotto
▷ Roast wild boar
Mixed dried fruit in spiced wine and Kirsch

1 *To prepare the marinade*: Mix together in a large china bowl the red wine, the vinegar, bay leaf, juniper berries (bruised), cinnamon, sage, onion, peeled carrot, celery stalk and peeled, thinly sliced garlic; add a little salt and freshly ground pepper.

2 Place the meat in the marinade; cover and leave to stand for 3 days in a cool place, turning at intervals.

3 Remove the meat from the marinade. Strain the marinade and reserve. Sauté the diced bacon in butter in a heavy-bottomed saucepan. Drain and dry off the meat and add to bacon.

4 Brown the meat over a fairly high heat for 15 to 20 minutes, turning frequently; add the hot broth and half the marinade a little at a time and continue cooking.

5 When this liquid has reduced add the washed, sliced mushrooms.

6 Cover and cook for 1½ hours in the oven, preheated to 350°F, basting the meat at frequent intervals with the remaining strained marinade.

7 Remove the meat and set aside, covered to retain the heat. Mix 1 teaspoon of potato flour with the cream in a bowl and add to the mushrooms, stirring over low heat with a wooden spoon.

8 When the sauce is smooth and has thickened, carve the wild boar meat into fairly thick chunks and cover with the sauce. Serve with slices of baked polenta lightly browned under a very hot broiler.

Haunch of venison with redcurrant sauce

Preparation and cooking time: About 2 hours

Serves 6: A 2¾ lb haunch of venison ● 5 juniper berries ● pinch of thyme ● pinch of marjoram ● 1 teaspoon finely chopped chives ● ¼ cup oil ● 1 small onion, finely chopped ● 3 tablespoons red wine vinegar ● 1 cup dry red wine ● 1 tablespoon redcurrant jelly ● 1 cup sour cream ● salt ● pepper

Suggested wines

Pommard, Taurasi, Teroldego

Suggested menu

Cream of lettuce soup
▷ Haunch of venison with redcurrant sauce
Fresh fruit mosaic

1 Rub the haunch of venison all over with the crushed juniper berries, sprinkle with a little salt, freshly ground pepper and the herbs.

2 Heat the oil in a large cooking pot. Place the venison in the hot oil and brown evenly.

3 Add the chopped onion, the wine, vinegar and a few tablespoons of hot water. Cover and continue cooking over moderate heat for $1\frac{1}{2}$ hours, turning from time to time and basting with the cooking juices.

4 When the venison is done, remove from the pot and keep warm. Strain the cooking juices through a fine sieve.

5 Add the redcurrant jelly and the sour cream to the strained juices, mixing well.

6 Pour this sauce over the venison and serve at once.

In Europe this dish would be made with roe-buck, which is considered better eating than the red deer (the recipe on page 58 calls for the latter, which needs marinating to tenderize it and give it flavor). For this dish, an animal shot at an unsuspecting moment will be more tender than game that is chased. However, you should not attempt this recipe unless you are sure that the animal was above the minimum age required by law when killed.

Extra special terrine

Preparation and cooking time: 1 hour 50 minutes

Serves 4: 1¼ cups finely chopped or ground pork ●
1 cup finely chopped or ground beef ● ½ cup finely
minced chicken ● 1 cup chicken livers ● 6 oz fresh
pork fat ● pinch of thyme ● 1 bay leaf ● 1 tablespoon
shelled pistachio nuts ● 2 chicken breasts ●
3 tablespoons brandy ● 3 tablespoons Madeira ●
3 tablespoons sherry ● 2 tablespoons butter ● salt ●
pepper

Serve with a little chopped aspic jelly (*see* recipe,
p 175), gherkins and hot French bread

Suggested wines

Marsala, sherry

Suggested menu

Cream of shrimp soup
▷ Extra special terrine
Apples flamed in rum

66

1 Cut the two chicken breasts into four fillets. Place in a dish with two-thirds of the fresh pork fat cut in strips. Pour over the sherry and Madeira and leave for 30 minutes.

2 Melt the butter in a cast-iron skillet, add half the chicken livers and sauté, seasoning with salt and pepper; sprinkle with the brandy and cook until this has evaporated.

3 Blend the remaining diced pork fat and chicken livers until almost a paste. Transfer to a bowl.

4 Remove the skin from the pistachio nuts by pouring boiling water on them and draining immediately; the skins will then rub off. Chop finely and season.

5 Mix the nuts, chicken liver paste, ground pork, beef and minced chicken into a smooth, even mixture.

6 Butter a rectangular terrine, cover the bottom with a layer of the ground meat and nut mixture; place two chicken fillets flat on top of this, together with a few strips of pork fat. Cover with another layer of mixture. Use a piping bag to layer the meat mixture if you like.

7 Arrange the sautéed chicken livers in a line down the center.

8 Cover with another layer of meat mixture and continue layering until all the ingredients have been used. Sprinkle with a little thyme, press the bay leaf into the surface and cover the terrine. Place in a roasting pan half-filled with boiling water (place a dish towel on the bottom of the roasting pan). Cook for about 1 hour at 375°F. Allow to cool completely before cutting into slices.

Couscous

Preparation and cooking time: About 2½ hours

Serves 8–10: A 2¾–3 lb fresh chicken, boned and cut into pieces ● 3–3½ lb mutton (neck and shoulder, boned and cut into cubes) ● 1 cup chick-peas, presoaked and parboiled ● 8 ripe tomatoes ● ½ lb pumpkin flesh (rind and seeds removed) ● 6 medium-sized onions, sliced ● 1 sachet saffron ● ⅓ cup seedless white raisins (presoaked in warm water) ● 3¼ cups coarse semolina ● ½ cup butter ● 2 cloves ● pinch of mixed spice ● pinch of chili powder ● salt ● pepper

Suggested wines

Chiaretto del Garda, Rosé de Provence, Bourgogne blanc

Suggested menu

▷ Couscous
Pear and walnut cake

1 Bring 2 quarts water to a boil in a large saucepan. Rub the chicken and mutton with salt and pepper and add to the boiling water with the onions, chili powder, mixed spice, cloves, a knob of butter and the chick-peas.

2 Pour the semolina on to a large shallow plate and sprinkle with a cup of salted water. Work it over so all is evenly moistened.

3 Continue to knead the semolina. If too damp, add a little more semolina.

4 Sieve the semolina once it has amalgamated into small pellets. Spread out on a clean dish towel. Dry in the oven, at 250°F with the door open.

5 Add the chopped tomatoes and pumpkin flesh to the ingredients that have been boiling.

6 Spread the dish towel with the semolina inside a metal colander. Fold over the edges and place over the boiling meat and vegetables. Cover tightly and steam for 30 minutes.

7 Turn the semolina onto a large plate and separate any pellets that have stuck together. Sprinkle with a little cold water, mix very gently and sprinkle again.

8 After about 2 hours, when the meat is tender, remove from heat and drop in the seedless white raisins tied up in a cheesecloth; add the saffron and return to the heat. Replace the semolina in the colander and steam for 5 more minutes. Spread on a heated serving platter, dot with butter and gradually sprinkle with the stock from the meat. Arrange the meat and vegetables on the semolina. Serve the remaining stock separately.

Milanese mixed fry

Preparation and cooking time: 3 hours

Serves 6: 3 calves' brains ● 12 pieces spinal cord
(optional) ● 14 oz calves' hearts ● $\frac{3}{4}$ lb or 6 veal
escalopes ● 6 very thin slices calves' liver ● 2 calves'
kidneys ● 12 calves' sweetbreads ● 12 potato
croquettes (made with 12 tablespoons firm mashed
potatoes, 1 egg, pinch of nutmeg, salt and pepper) ●
1 tablespoon wine vinegar ● $\frac{1}{4}$ onion ● 2 zucchinis ●
3 young fresh or canned artichokes ● 12 florets
cauliflower ● juice of 3 lemons ● 2–3 tablespoons
chopped parsley ● 6 tablespoons meat gravy or stock
● butter ● oil ● breadcrumbs ● 12 eggs, lightly beaten
● salt ● pepper

Suggested wines

Bardolino, Beaujolais Villages, Moulin-à-vent

Suggested menu

▷ Milanese mixed fry
Rainbow salad
Grapes with pink cream

1 *To prepare the brains*: Leave to soak in a bowl of cold water for 30 minutes. Blanch for 5 minutes in water that has been brought to the boil with the ¼ onion, salt and vinegar. Drain and refresh under cold running water; use a small, sharp knife to pull and trim away any membrane and then cut into large cubes. Place in a bowl and sprinkle with a little lemon juice and some of the chopped parsley. Roll gently in flour, dip in the beaten egg and then fry in hot butter.

2 *To prepare the spinal cord*: Pull the meat out of the skin and poach briefly in lightly salted water (about 1 minute); drain, rinse in cold water and pat dry with paper towels. Flour lightly, dip in beaten egg and sauté in hot butter.

3 *To prepare the calves' hearts*: Slice thinly and boil for 5 minutes in salted water; drain, dry and flour lightly then fry in plenty of very hot oil.

4 *To prepare the veal escalopes*: Flatten slightly with a meat mallet rinsed in cold water; dip in the beaten egg, coat with breadcrumbs, dip once more into the beaten egg and season with salt and freshly ground pepper. Fry until golden brown, drain and sprinkle with lemon juice and chopped parsley.

5 *To prepare the livers*: Dust the liver with flour and fry for a few minutes only, in the hot oil.

6 *To prepare the kidneys*: Slice the kidneys removing any membrane and sauté briefly in hot butter. Season with salt and pepper.

7 *To prepare the sweetbreads*: Leave to

soak for 30 minutes in cold water; drain and blanch for up to 5 minutes. Allow to cool in the cooking water, then drain and trim off any membrane before cutting into cubes. Roll in flour, dip in the beaten egg and sauté in hot butter until golden brown.

8 *To prepare the potato croquettes*: Place 12 tablespoons mashed potatoes in a bowl and beat in the egg; season with a pinch of salt, nutmeg and pepper, mix and shape into 12 croquettes. Dip into the beaten egg, coat with breadcrumbs and deep fry in boiling oil; remove when they are crisp and golden brown.

9 *To prepare the zucchini*: Trim off ends, wash, dry and then slice lengthwise. Coat with flour and fry in very hot oil.

10 *To prepare the artichokes*: Trim, wash and boil the artichokes in salted water for 10 minutes and then cut each one into four. Dip in beaten egg and deep fry in plenty of boiling oil. Remove with a slotted spoon and drain well.

11 *To prepare the cauliflower florets*: Wash, boil in salted water for 10 minutes or until just tender; drain and dry with paper towels. Dip in beaten egg and fry in hot butter until golden brown.

12 Arrange all the fried ingredients on a heated serving diih; sprinkle with a little lemon juice and chopped parsley.

13 Heat 2 tablespoons of butter in a small saucepan until light golden brown.

14 Sprinkle the mixed fry with the butter and the hot meat gravy or stock.

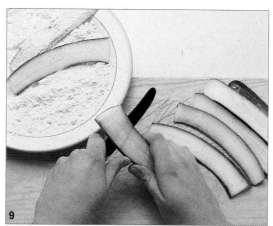

This mixed fry or *fritto misto* is a classic Italian dish, although the ingredients vary from region to region. The version we have chosen comes from Milan and is one of the most popular.

Poultry and feathered game

Chicken en croûte

Suggested wines

Viña Ardanza, Côtes du Rhône Villages, Nebbiolo

Suggested menu

Special sweet corn soup
▷ Chicken en croûte
Pears Cardinal

Preparation and cooking time: 1 hour 10 minutes

Serves 4: A 3½–4 lb chicken ● 4 oz chicken livers ●
1 onion ● 1 clove garlic ● 6 medium-sized mushrooms
● ¾ cup dry white wine ● 1½ tablespoons butter ●
½ cup boiled rice ● 1 bay leaf ● 1 egg yolk ●
1 cup chicken stock ● salt ● pepper

For the pastry: 1¼ cups flour ● ½ cup + 2 tablespoons
butter ● 1 egg

To prepare the chicken: Use a very sharp knife and
poultry scissors to cut the whole of the breast neatly
away, leaving the rest of the chicken whole. Remove
the bone and cartilage from the breast, carefully pull off
the strip of white gristle on the inside of each breast and
open out flat. Remove the carcass, leaving the thigh
bones. Pound the breasts lightly with a meat mallet and
set aside. Heat the butter in a heavy-bottomed casserole
dish, place the whole chicken in the casserole and
brown all over at high heat. When browned, season
with salt and freshly ground pepper, remove chicken
from the casserole and keep hot.

1 Pour the cooking juices
and fat that remain from
browning the chicken into
a skillet and add the finely
chopped onion and garlic,
the sliced mushrooms,
rice, the chopped chicken
livers and the bay leaf;
cook gently for a few
minutes. Pour in the white
wine and cook for a few
minutes longer. Add a
little stock as the wine
evaporates.

2 Place the browned
chicken on a buttered
roasting pan. Fill the
cavity of the chicken with
the rice and chicken liver
mixture and cover with
the breast pieces.

3 Place the flour in a
large mixing bowl, cut the
butter into small pieces
and rub into the flour,
adding a pinch of salt;
gradually work in the
lightly beaten egg.

4 Roll out the pastry.

5 Cover the chicken with
the pastry, cut away the
excess and reserve for
decoration. Tuck the
pastry well underneath the
edges of the chicken.

6 Use the pastry
trimmings to cut out
leaves and press gently on
the pastry case. Brush the
surface with beaten egg
yolk and bake in a
preheated oven at 350°F
for 40 minutes.

Chicken in cream sauce

Preparation and cooking time: 1 hour 45 minutes

Serves 4: A 3½–4 lb chicken ● 20 baby onions, peeled
● 2 cups button mushrooms ● juice of ½ lemon ●
1¾ cups chicken stock ● pinch of grated nutmeg ●
1 pint cream ● 2 tablespoons butter ● salt ● pepper

For the sauce: 3 tablespoons butter ● 1 pint chicken
stock ● 1½ tablespoons flour ● salt ● pepper

Suggested wines

Chianti, Châteauneuf-du-Pape, Pomerol

Suggested menu

Bosun's noodles
▷ Chicken in cream sauce
Chilled peach and rum soufflés

1 Trim and wash the mushrooms, place in a bowl and sprinkle with the lemon juice.

2 Wash and dry the chicken and cut into small serving pieces.

3 Melt the butter in a large, heavy-bottomed skillet and brown the chicken pieces briskly over fairly high heat; season with salt and freshly ground pepper. Add the mushrooms and the baby onions; pour in 1½ cups stock and continue cooking over lower heat for about 30 minutes, turning the chicken every now and then.

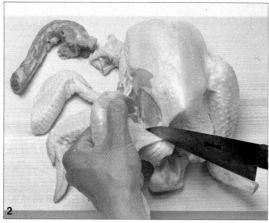

4 While the chicken is cooking, make the sauce. Melt the butter in a saucepan and add the flour, stirring constantly to prevent lumps; season with a little salt and pepper.

5 Stir in the hot chicken stock a little at a time and continue cooking until the sauce is smooth and creamy.

6 Add the cooked chicken to the sauce; pour in the cream, season with a pinch of grated nutmeg and stir. Simmer for a few minutes and then transfer to a deep hot serving dish.

This recipe works equally well with veal or turkey (pound briefly with a meat mallet before cutting into small pieces). Serve with pilaf rice (see p. 176) to make a complete one-course meal.

New Castile chicken with apples

Preparation and cooking time: 1 hour 45 minutes

Serves 4: A 3½–4 lb chicken ● 2 apples ● juice of
1 lemon ● 3 tablespoons marc (brandy) or Grappa ●
5 oz sliced bacon or salt pork (*pancetta*) ● ¾ cup dry
white wine ● 6 tablespoons oil ● a few coarsely ground
peppercorns ● salt ● pepper

Suggested wines

Dôle du Mont, Château Paveil de Luze, Chianti

Suggested menu

Country style pasta
▷ New Castile chicken with apples
Pineapple rings in rum custard

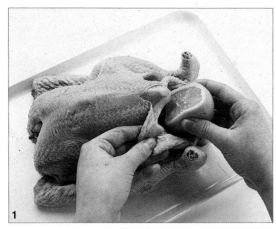

1 Wash and dry the chicken and season the cavity with a pinch of salt, the coarsely ground peppercorns and the lemon juice.

2 Wash, peel and core the apples, dip in acidulated water if wished to prevent them from discoloring, and cut one in half. Push one half well down into the chicken's cavity, followed by the whole apple and then by the remaining half.

3 Sew up the opening or secure with a skewer; sprinkle the chicken with a little salt and pepper and wrap the slices of bacon or *pancetta* around it, securing with small skewers.

4 Place the chicken in a casserole dish with the oil and cook in a hot oven (400°F), turning once or twice so that it browns evenly; after 30 minutes mix the marc or Grappa with the wine and pour over the chicken.

5 Continue cooking for another 40–50 minutes or until the meat is tender and the juices run clear when the thigh is pierced with a knife. Baste frequently with the cooking juices and oil.

6 When the chicken is cooked, cut into four pieces and serve at once, garnishing each serving with half an apple.

Oriental Rock Cornish hens

Preparation and cooking time: 1 hour 10 minutes

Serves 4: 2 Rock Cornish hens, cleaned • 1 can dried chestnuts • generous $\frac{1}{4}$ cup butter • $\frac{3}{4}$ cup dry white wine • $\frac{3}{4}$ cup cream • $1\frac{1}{4}$ lb bacon or salted smoked belly of pork • 1 small onion • 1 cup fine fresh breadcrumbs • juice of $\frac{1}{2}$ lemon • 3 sage leaves, chopped • 1 tablespoon tomato paste • 6 tablespoons stock • 6 tablespoons grated Parmesan cheese • 1 bay leaf • scant $\frac{3}{4}$ cup Marsala (sweet dessert wine) • $\frac{1}{4}$ stock cube • heaping teaspoon cornstarch • scant 1 cup oil • nutmeg • salt • pepper

Garnish: chopped parsley, watercress

Serve with chestnut purée (see recipe, p. 175) and asparagus wrapped in smoked ham strips

Suggested wines

Cabernet d'Anjou, Château Latour, Barbaresco

Suggested menu

Black olive canapés
▷ Oriental Rock Cornish hens
Almond ice cream with chocolate rum sauce

1 Simmer the dried chestnuts for a few minutes then set aside.

2 Chop the onion finely with the bacon and fry in 2 tablespoons of butter with the bay leaf.

3 Add the breadcrumbs, grated Parmesan and lemon juice and mix well.

4 Stir in 1 teaspoon tomato paste followed by about two-thirds of the drained chestnuts. Crush them into the mixture with a fork. Season with salt, grated nutmeg, pepper and the sage leaves.

5 Cut the hens in half and pound flat with the meat mallet. Heat the oil in a very large skillet and fry each halved hen over high heat for 15 minutes, turning frequently. Season, and moisten with a little white wine.

6 Place each halved hen on a chopping board and cover with a few spoonfuls of the chestnut, cheese and breadcrumb mixture; press one or two of the reserved chestnuts on top. Sprinkle with a little grated Parmesan. Place in the oven (preheated to 350°F) and cook for 10–15 minutes or until golden brown.

7 Make the sauce. Work the cornstarch into the remaining softened butter and stir into the cooking juices in the pan. Stir in the remaining tomato paste mixed with the stock and cook over low heat; when the sauce has thickened slightly, add the Marsala and cream. Crumble the extra stock cube into the sauce and mix well; simmer, stirring constantly, for about 10 minutes. Serve at once, spooning a little sauce on to each plate and placing half a hen on top. Serve any remaining sauce separately.

Dried chestnuts can be found in delicatessens or in Chinese or Japanese grocery stores.

Turkish roast chicken

Preparation and cooking time: 2 hours 30 minutes

Serves 4: A 3½–4lb chicken ● 5 celery stalks ● 2 large cloves garlic ● 1 tomato ● 1 carrot ● ¾ cup dry white wine ● 4 tablespoons oil ● ¼ cup butter ● ¾ cup water ● salt ● pepper.

Garnish: a few radishes.

Serve with steamed cauliflower and broccoli

Suggested wines

Cabernet del Collio, Oltrepò Pavese, Pauillac

Suggested menu

Celery stuffed with salmon mousse
▷ Turkish roast chicken
Strawberry Bavarian cream

1 Wash and dry the chicken, season the cavity with salt and freshly ground pepper and place two stalks of celery inside.

2 Rub the chicken with the crushed cloves of garlic; pour over the oil.

3 Sprinkle the chicken on the outside with salt and freshly ground pepper.

4 Truss the chicken securely, making sure that the opening is firmly tied.

5 Wash and trim the vegetables; peel the carrot, cut lengthwise in four; cut the celery stalks in half and quarter the tomato.

6 Transfer the chicken to a roasting pan and surround by the vegetables. Pour in the water.

7 Place the butter on top of the chicken and place in the oven, preheated to 400°F. Roast for 1½–2 hours, basting the chicken frequently with the liquid in the pan and adding a little white wine each time this is done. Add a little boiling water during cooking, if necessary. Half-way through the roasting time, turn the chicken so that it browns evenly. When the chicken is cooked, remove the trussing string and transfer to a heated serving platter. Liquidize the cooking juices and vegetables cooked with the chicken in a blender and serve this sauce separately.

Serve the chicken with steamed cauliflower and broccoli.

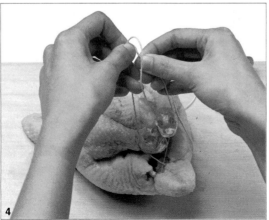

Chicken Waterzooi

Preparation and cooking time: 1 hour 20 minutes

Serves 4: A 3 lb chicken cut into serving pieces •
1 large white onion • 3 celery hearts • 3 large leeks
(green tops removed) • 6¼ cups veal stock (made from
raw veal, 1 onion, 2 small carrots, 1 stick celery, a
bouquet garni and 2 peppercorns) • 3 egg yolks •
1 tablespoon finely chopped parsley • 3 tablespoons
grated Parmesan cheese • 1 tablespoon unsalted butter
• 1½ teaspoons cornstarch • salt

Serve with triangles of bread fried in butter

Suggested wines

Inferno, Nuits-Saint-Georges, Taurasi

Suggested menu

▷ Chicken Waterzooi
Coffee flavored ratafia cream

1 Wash the celery hearts and the trimmed white part of the leeks; dry before slicing into thin strips.

2 Butter a deep, heavy-bottomed enamel pot; place the celery, leeks and chopped onion in the bottom and then place the chicken pieces on top. Cover the chicken with veal stock.

3 Place a circle of buttered wax paper over the pot and seal firmly with the lid. Bring slowly to a boil, lower the heat and simmer gently for an hour. Remove from the heat, take up the chicken pieces and transfer to a heated dish. Cover and keep warm.

4 Beat the egg yolks with the chopped parsley and add the grated Parmesan cheese. Trickle the hot stock from the pot, reserving the vegetables, in a thin stream onto the beaten egg yolks, whisking vigorously.

5 Mix 1½ teaspoons of cornstarch together with a little water or stock and add to the liquid, stirring well. Return this mixture to the heat and simmer gently, stirring constantly, for about 10 minutes or until the sauce has become creamy and thick.

6 Pour the sauce over the chicken pieces and vegetables, arranged in a tureen and serve immediately with the pieces of bread fried in butter.

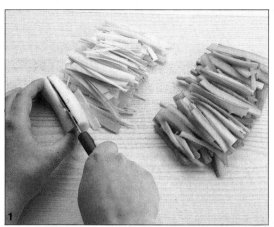

This well-known Belgian dish is traditionally served on special occasions. There is an equally popular version using fish.

Spicy tomato chicken

Preparation and cooking time: 1 hour 30 minutes

Serves 4: A 3½–4 lb chicken ● 4 large onions ● 2 large crisp apples ● ½ cup butter ● 1 level tablespoonful tomato paste ● 5 tablespoons coconut milk ● ¾ cup thick cream ● 2 tablespoon lemon juice ● a pinch of powdered bay leaf ● a pinch of thyme ● a pinch of cinnamon ● 1 pint chicken stock ● salt ● pepper ● ½ tablespoon garam masala

Suggested wines

Montilla Cobos, Pinot nero del Collio, Pommard

Suggested menu

▷ Spicy tomato chicken
Exotic fruit salad

1 Wash the chicken, dry and cut into serving pieces.

2 Melt the butter in a large, heavy-bottomed saucepan over moderate heat; add the sliced onions, the apples, peeled cored and chopped, and the cinnamon. Fry gently for 5 minutes.

3 Add the chicken portions and brown for 5 minutes, stirring and turning frequently.

4 Add the chicken stock, a pinch of salt, a little freshly ground pepper, the thyme and powdered bay leaf and simmer gently for 30 minutes.

5 Sprinkle in the garam masala and add the tomato paste mixed with the coconut milk. Continue cooking over low heat for 8–10 minutes, until the sauce has reduced and thickened slightly.

6 Just before serving, stir in the cream, mixed with the lemon juice. Reheat gently and serve with basmati rice.

Tunisian chicken

Preparation and cooking time: 1 hour 30 minutes

Serves 4: A 3½–4 lb chicken ● ⅔ cup oil ● ¾ cup pitted green olives ● 1 teaspoon anchovy paste (made by crushing 1–2 anchovy fillets into a smooth paste) ● 1½ cups canned tomatoes ● 1 clove garlic ● salt ● pepper

Suggested wines

Côte de Brouilly, Cabernet di Pramaggiore, Santa Maddalena

Suggested menu

Vegetable and cheese quiche
▷ Tunisian chicken
Moist date cake

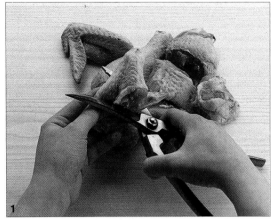

1 Wash and dry the chicken and cut into serving pieces.

2 Heat the oil in a large, heavy-bottomed saucepan and brown the chicken pieces all over, turning frequently so that they cook evenly. Season with a little salt and freshly ground pepper. When the chicken is browned, take up the pieces and keep warm.

3 Place the tomatoes in a large, deep skillet, crushing them with a fork to break them up. Stir in the anchovy paste and a couple of spoonfuls of water and simmer for a few minutes.

4 Add the whole peeled garlic clove, then the chicken pieces followed by the olives.

5 Simmer over low heat for 30–40 minutes, stirring now and then and add a few spoonfuls of hot water if the sauce reduces too rapidly.

6 Remove and discard the garlic; place the chicken portions on a heated serving platter and cover with the sauce. Serve at once.

Chicken Florentine

Preparation and cooking time: 1 hour 10 minutes

Serves 4: A 2¼ lb chicken ● ¼ cup butter ● ¾ cup dry white wine ● 1 cup chicken stock ● half a lemon ● 2 lb fresh spinach, lightly boiled ● 1 pint cream ● 3 hard-boiled eggs ● 6 tablespoons freshly grated Parmesan cheese ● 1 tablespoon finely chopped parsley ● salt ● pepper

For the sauce: ¼ cup flour ● 2 tablespoons butter ● 1 cup milk ● a pinch of grated nutmeg ● 2 egg yolks ● salt ● pepper

Suggested wines

Chianti, Pomerol, Pinot nero dell'Alto Adige

Suggested menu

Ham, egg and cheese risotto
▷ Chicken Florentine
Coffee flavored ratafia cream

1 Wash and dry the chicken and cut in half. Melt half the butter in a skillet. Pour in the white wine and season with a little salt and freshly ground pepper. Add the chicken, the stock and 1¼ cups of cream; simmer gently for 20 minutes. Test the chicken to see if it is cooked (the juices should run clear when the meat is pierced at its thickest point).

2 Take up the chicken halves, remove the bones and cut the meat into slices. Cover with foil and keep warm. Reserve the juices in the skillet.

3 Melt the remaining butter in a pan or casserole dish and stir in the well-drained, coarsely chopped spinach. Add the remaining cream, season with a little salt and pepper.

4 *To prepare the sauce*: Melt the butter, and add the flour, stirring vigorously to prevent lumps. Pour in the milk, and stir until the sauce thickens. Add the salt, pepper and nutmeg and cook for about 4–5 minutes stirring constantly. Add this sauce to the reserved liquid in the skillet and stir in the juice of half a lemon.

5 Beat the egg yolks briefly and trickle into the sauce, stirring constantly until the sauce thickens.

6 Spoon a portion of spinach onto four individual ovenproof plates, top with chicken slices and cover with the sauce. Sprinkle with grated Parmesan cheese and place in the oven, preheated to 350°F, for 10 minutes, to brown. Garnish each serving with slices of hard-boiled egg and chopped parsley and serve at once.

This nourishing and easily digested dish makes an excellent light supper meal and goes well with piping hot creamed potatoes.

Curried chicken casserole

Preparation and cooking time: 1 hour 10 minutes

Serves 4: 4 chicken breasts ● 4 large mushrooms ●
1 onion ● 1 clove garlic ● 1 egg yolk ● 1 cup dry
white wine ● $\frac{1}{4}$ cup butter ● 2 peeled, boiled potatoes
● $2\frac{1}{2}$ cups milk ● $\frac{1}{2}$ cup flour ● 3 tablespoons grated
Parmesan cheese ● 1 tablespoon curry powder ● salt
● pepper

Suggested wines

Dôle du Mont, Valpolicella, Pauillac

Suggested menu

Tuna and avocado appetizer
▷ Curried chicken casserole
Cherries à la mode

1 Peel and slice the onion, dice the chicken breasts; wash, dry and slice the mushrooms.

2 Melt the butter in a deep skillet and gently fry the diced chicken, onion and finely chopped garlic.

3 Pour in the wine and continue cooking until it has evaporated. Season with salt and freshly ground pepper and then take up the chicken, mushrooms and onion with a slotted spoon, and keep warm. Leave the cooking juices in the pan.

4 Stir the flour into the juices and fat and add the curry powder.

5 Heat the milk to just below boiling point and gradually add to the curry mixture, stirring constantly.

6 Simmer for 5–10 minutes, stirring or whisking until the sauce is smooth and creamy.

7 Meanwhile, boil the potatoes and push through a sieve or mash into a bowl. Stir in the egg yolk and season with salt and freshly ground pepper, mixing very thoroughly.

8 Butter a deep casserole dish and cover the bottom with one-third of the chicken mixture; cover with half the sauce and sprinkle with half the grated Parmesan cheese. Arrange the rest of the chicken mixture on top and cover with the remaining sauce and cheese. Put a fluted nozzle on a piping bag and spoon the mashed potatoes into the bag; pipe a decorative border around the edge of the dish. Place under a hot broiler until the top is a pale golden brown. Serve straight from the casserole dish while very hot.

Chicken liver mousse

Preparation and cooking time: 1 hour 30 minutes

Serves 4: 9 chicken livers • 6 tablespoons unsalted pork fat • 2 eggs • $\frac{2}{3}$ cup fresh breadcrumbs • 1 clove garlic • 1 tablespoon finely chopped parsley • $\frac{3}{4}$ cup heavy cream • 2 tablespoons butter • $\frac{3}{4}$ cup brandy • $\frac{3}{4}$ cup port • 1 tablespoon chopped chives • $2\frac{1}{4}$ cups canned tomatoes • 1 onion • 6 tablespoons oil • salt • pepper

Suggested wines

Pinot d'Alsace, Riesling dell'Oltrepò Pavese, Saint-Estèphe

Suggested menu

▷ Chicken liver mousse
Roast veal with mixed herbs
Peaches and apricots in citrus syrup

1 Wash and trim the chicken livers, using a very sharp pointed knife to cut away any pieces of gristle and membrane.

2 Place in a bowl and cover with cold water; leave to stand for 30 minutes.

3 Drain and chop the livers and cover with the brandy.

4 Chop the pork fat very finely.

5 Place the chicken livers and brandy in a blender or food processor together with the port, eggs and breadcrumbs. Season generously with salt and freshly ground pepper. Blend until the mixture is very smooth and transfer to a bowl. Whisk in the parsley, the finely chopped garlic and the cream.

6 Brush the inside of four ramekins or molds with melted butter.

7 Spoon equal quantities of the mixture into the ramekins or molds. Place on a cookie sheet and cook in the oven in a *bain-marie* at 320°F for 40 minutes.

8 While the mousses are cooking, make the tomato sauce. Sauté the chopped onion in the oil until pale golden brown; add the tomatoes and break up coarsely with a fork. Season with salt and freshly ground pepper and simmer gently until the sauce has reduced and thickened. Remove from heat and push through a sieve. Turn the mousses out carefully onto individual heated plates. Spoon 3 tablespoons of tomato sauce over each; sprinkle with chopped chives and serve very hot.

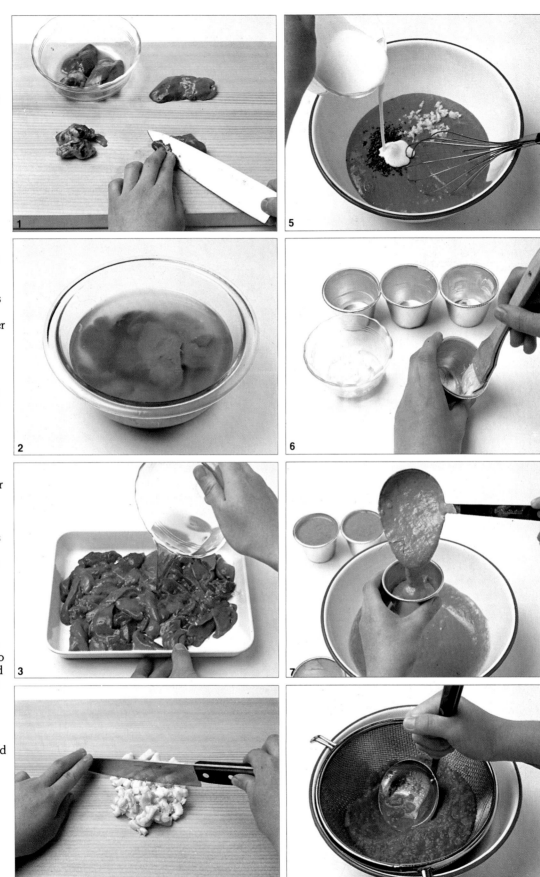

Duck à l'orange

Preparation and cooking time: 2 hours

Serves 4: A 4 lb duck ● ½ cup butter ● 2 oranges ●
peel of 1 orange ● 1 cup light stock ● 1½ tablespoons
potato flour or cornstarch ● ¾ cup dry sherry ●
3 tablespoons Curaçao ● salt ● pepper

Suggested wines

Cabernet del Collio, Pommard, Pinot noir Napa
Valley

Suggested menu

Mushroom and ham rice timbale
▷ Duck à l'orange
Almond ice cream with chocolate rum sauce

96

1 Wash the duck and dry well. Place a small piece of butter inside the cavity and rub a little butter over the less fatty parts of the breast; season inside and out with salt and freshly ground pepper. Pierce skin all over with a fork.

2 Place the duck on a rack in a large roasting pan in an oven preheated to 425°F, turning the heat down to 350°F after 15 minutes. A 4 lb duck will take about 1½ hours total cooking time. Alternatively, cook over direct heat in a large deep saucepan. Pierce the breast with the prongs of a fork; when they slide in easily, remove the duck from the roasting pan and keep warm. Reserve the cooking juices.

3 *To prepare the orange sauce*: Pare off the rind of an orange, leaving behind the pith. Blanch in boiling water for a few minutes.

4 Drain off the water, dry the rind and cut into very thin strips; place in a bowl with the Curaçao. Pour the boiling stock into the juices in the roasting pan. Stir in the potato flour or cornstarch mixed with the sherry and cook over high heat until the liquid has reduced by about one-third.

5 Add the orange peel and Curaçao and leave to simmer, stirring occasionally, for about 5–10 minutes. Remove from heat.

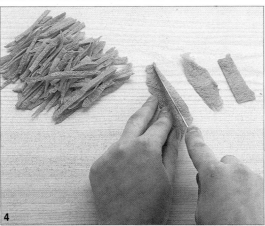

6 Peel the other oranges, removing all the pith, membrane and seeds from each segment.

7 Cut the duck into pieces and arrange on a heated serving platter; pour over the orange sauce and decorate with the orange segments.

This simplified version of the classic French dish makes a spectacular main course for a special dinner party. Garnish with triangles of bread fried in butter arranged around the edge of the serving dish.

Spanish almond duck

Preparation and cooking time: 2 hours

Serves 4: A 4 lb duck with its liver ● a few spoonfuls flour ● ½ cup fresh pork fat or shortening ● 2 shallots ● 1½ cups canned tomatoes ● 24 almonds ● 1 clove garlic ● small bunch parsley ● 1 cup dry white wine ● salt ● pepper

Suggested wines

Pommard, Chianti, Médoc

Suggested menu

Ham, egg and cheese risotto
▷ Spanish almond duck
Chocolate bananas

1 Wash the duck, dry thoroughly and chop into serving pieces. Reserve the liver as it is an essential part of this recipe.

2 Melt the finely chopped pork fat in a large, heavy-bottomed saucepan and when it is hot sauté the finely chopped duck's liver for 2 or 3 minutes. Remove with a slotted spoon and keep warm.

3 Sauté the finely sliced shallots until a very pale golden brown, remove these with a slotted spoon and keep warm with the liver.

4 Coat the duck pieces with flour and brown well in the hot fat; season with salt and freshly ground pepper.

5 Add the roughly chopped tomatoes and simmer for about 1 hour, turning and stirring from time to time.

6 Toast the almonds in the oven until light golden brown, then chop them up with the cooked liver, shallots and garlic; place in a bowl and moisten with white wine.

7 Add this mixture to the simmering duck and tomatoes, stir and continue cooking, covered, for about 40 minutes. Serve the duck in its sauce, sprinkled with finely chopped parsley.

When cooked in this traditional Spanish style, the duck remains moist and tender and has a particularly delicate flavor.

Pheasant à la géorgienne

Preparation and cooking time: 1 hour 30 minutes

Serves 4: A plump young hen pheasant ● 12 strips barding fat (bacon or salt pork) ● 20 walnuts ● 1¾ lb white grapes ● ¾ cup strained green tea ● juice of 2 large oranges ● scant ¾ cup Marsala ● 3 tablespoons butter ● salt ● pepper

Suggested wines

Barbaresco, Cabernet Sauvignon Napa Valley, Saint-Emilion

Suggested menu

Asparagus and rice mold
▷ Pheasant à la géorgienne
Pears, figs and almonds in honey sauce

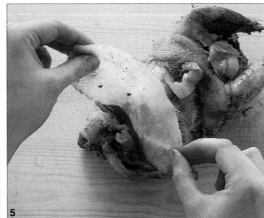

1 Wash and dry the pheasant; season the cavity with a little salt and freshly ground pepper.

2 Wrap the barding fat around the pheasant and secure with wooden skewers.

3 Place in a heavy-bottomed casserole with the butter, adding the orange juice and the chopped or coarsely broken up walnuts.

4 Place the grapes in a sieve and crush with a wooden spoon, collecting the juice in a bowl. Add to the casserole together with the Marsala followed by the green tea; cover and simmer for 40 minutes over gentle heat.

5 When cooked, take up the pheasant, remove the barding fat and return to the casserole to brown. Season with a little more salt and freshly ground pepper.

6 When the pheasant has browned, transfer to a heated serving dish and cover with the sauce.

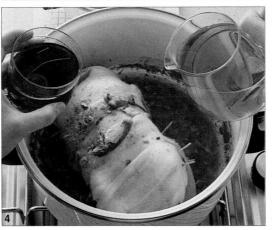

Hen pheasants generally have a more delicate flavor and are more tender than cock pheasants.

101

Roast goose with chestnuts and apples

Preparation and cooking time: 3 hours

Serves 4–6: A 4½–8 lb goose ● 14 oz peeled chestnuts
● 1½ pints brown stock ● a pinch of chopped tarragon
● 3 apples ● ⅓ cup seedless white raisins ●
2 tablespoons potato flour or cornstarch ● 6
tablespoons oil ● salt ● pepper

Suggested wines

Saint-Emilion, Moulin-à-vent, Inferno

Suggested menu

Pumpkin soup
▷ Roast goose with chestnuts and apples
Caramelized pears

1 Parboil the chestnuts in 1 pint of stock. Wash, quarter and core the apples. Soak the raisins in warm water.

2 Mix the drained chestnuts with the apple quarters and the well-drained raisins.

3 Wash, dry and season the goose inside and out with salt, freshly ground pepper and tarragon. Fill the cavity with the fruit and chestnut stuffing.

4 Sew up the opening and place the goose in a roasting pan that has been greased with a tablespoon of oil.

5 Place in a hot oven, preheated to 400°F and roast for about 2½–3 hours. Baste from time to time with a little of the remaining hot stock and turn the bird at intervals.

6 When the goose is cooked, transfer it from the roasting pan onto a heated serving platter. Strain the cooking juices and liquid from the pan into a small saucepan; mix the potato flour or cornstarch with a little cold water, add to the saucepan and cook for about 5 minutes, stirring constantly. Pour over the goose.

This German recipe includes one of a tremendous variety of stuffings for roast goose from many parts of the world. You can stuff your bird with sausage meat and beans, sauerkraut and apples or vegetables and fruit. Extra cooking time is always allowed for roasting a stuffed bird.

Foie gras truffé en gelée

Preparation and cooking time: 1 hour + 3 hours for soaking the truffle

Serves 4: 1 large raw goose liver ● 1 truffle, preferably fresh ● 2 large thin slices fresh pork fat ● $\frac{1}{2}$ cup Cognac ● $\frac{1}{2}$ cup port ● 2 pints cold stock ● 1 pint chicken aspic ● salt ● pepper

For the chicken aspic: $\frac{1}{2}$ lb chicken wings ● 1 onion ● 1 celery stalk ● 1 tablespoon gelatine powder ● 2 pints water

Suggested wines

Sauternes, Malvasia delle Lipari, Picolit

Suggested menu

▷ Foie gras truffé en gelée
Chicken Madagascar
Chilled peach and rum soufflés

1 Wash the truffle and scrape off the rough skin with a small sharp knife or brush. Place in a small bowl.

2 Pour the port over the truffle, followed by the Cognac and season very lightly with a pinch of salt and a little freshly ground pepper. Leave to soak for 3 hours. *To prepare the chicken aspic*: Make chicken stock with the chicken trimmings, vegetables and the water, boiling gently until the liquid has reduced to 1 pint strained volume. Dissolve the gelatine in this (do not allow to boil again).

3 Make a small, deep incision all the way to the center of the liver and push the drained truffle into this pocket.

4 Wrap the slices of pork fat around the liver, tying with string.

5 Wrap the barded liver in cheesecloth and sew up securely with thread.

6 Place the liver in the cold stock and bring to a gentle boil; simmer gently for 20 minutes.

7 Turn off the heat and leave the liver to cool gradually in the cooking liquid; when it is cold, take up and unwrap, removing the fat.

8 Pour some of the chicken aspic into an oblong or oval terrine; cover and chill in the refrigerator until just set; place the sliced goose liver on top and cover with more aspic. Return to the refrigerator to set. Chop the remaining chilled aspic and use to garnish the dish.

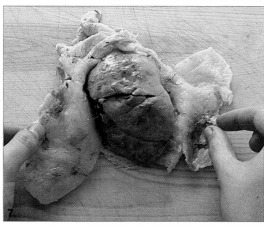

Piedmont quails

Preparation and cooking time: 1 hour 15 minutes

Serves 4: 8 quails ● 8 thin slices fresh pork fat ● $\frac{1}{4}$ cup butter ● small celery stalk ● a few spoonfuls light stock ● $\frac{3}{4}$ cup brandy ● 3 teaspoons truffle paste ● 1 scallion ● 1 carrot ● salt ● pepper

For the risotto: 2 cups risotto rice ● 3 tablespoons butter ● 3 tablespoons oil ● $1\frac{1}{2}$ pints light stock ● 1 finely chopped onion ● 4 tablespoons freshly grated Parmesan cheese ● $\frac{3}{4}$ cup dry white wine ● salt

Suggested wines

Nebbiolo, Moulin-à-vent, Beaujolais Villages

Suggested menu

▷ Piedmont quails
Orange semolina cream

1 Wash and dry the quails; season inside each with a pinch of salt, freshly ground pepper and a little truffle paste and sprinkle with the brandy.

2 Truss each bird and wrap in a piece of pork fat, securing with toothpicks.

3 Heat the butter in a large, heavy-bottomed saucepan and fry the quails together with the finely chopped scallion, celery and carrot.

4 Cook the quails over gentle heat for about 50 minutes, adding a few spoonfuls of stock to moisten every now and then.

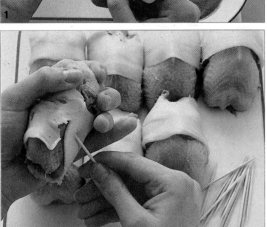

5 *To prepare the risotto*: While the quails are cooking, heat 2 tablespoons of the butter and the oil in a deep skillet and sauté the finely chopped onion gently until it is a very pale golden brown.

6 Add the rice and stir well so that the grains absorb the flavors of the butter, oil and onion. Pour in the white wine and stir until it has been absorbed or has evaporated.

7 Add about a cupful of boiling stock and continue cooking, adding more hot stock whenever it is needed. Make sure the rice does not stick to the bottom of the pan. Add a little salt if necessary.

8 When the rice is tender but still firm and the risotto is very moist, turn off the heat and stir in the grated Parmesan cheese and the remaining butter. Transfer to a heated serving platter; remove the barding fat from the birds and place on top of the risotto. Pour the remaining cooking liquid over the quails and serve piping hot.

Stuffed braised pigeons

Preparation and cooking time: About 1 hour

Serves 4: 4 plump young pigeons ● 4 slices of salt pork or bacon ● ¼ cup butter ● 3 tablespoons oil ● ¼ cup Cognac ● 1 bay leaf ● 5–6 tablespoons stock ● 1 teaspoon flour ● ½ cup cream ● salt ● pepper

For the stuffing: 1 cup ground beef ● ½ cup finely chopped calf's liver ● 2 oz ham or unsmoked bacon ● 2 sage leaves ● 2 eggs ● a few tablespoon fresh breadcrumbs ● 1½ tablespoons freshly grated Parmesan cheese ● ⅓ cup cream ● a few chopped fresh basil leaves (or pinch dried basil) ● half clove garlic ● salt ● pepper

Suggested wines

Médoc, Pommard, Chablis

Suggested menu

Pumpkin soup
▷ Stuffed braised pigeons
Bananas Martinique

1 Wash and dry the pigeons and season inside with a little salt and pepper. Mix all the stuffing ingredients together in a bowl and stuff the pigeons.

2 Sew up the openings and wrap each bird in a slice of the salt pork or bacon, securing with a toothpick. Place the pigeons in a heavy saucepan with the oil, 3 tablespoons of butter and a bay leaf. Fry until the birds have browned.

3 Season, sprinkle with Cognac and flame. When the flames have gone out, continue cooking the pigeons over

low heat for about 45 minutes, moistening occasionally with a few spoonfuls of hot stock.

4 When the pigeons are done, remove with a slotted spoon or tongs and keep hot. Make a *beurre manié* by working the remaining butter with the flour. Add to the cooking juices in the pan.

5 Cook slowly, stirring, and when the sauce has thickened, add the cream and simmer for 5 minutes.

6 Remove the barding bacon from the pigeons. Serve with creamed potatoes, and pour over the sauce.

Partridges in chocolate sauce

Preparation and cooking time: 1 hour 15 minutes

Serves 4: 4 well-hung medium-sized partridges ● $\frac{1}{2}$ cup olive oil ● 3 squares bitter (not semi-sweet) chocolate, grated ● 2 cloves garlic ● 6 tablespoons wine vinegar ● $\frac{1}{2}$ pint red wine ● 1 cup stock ● 1 bay leaf ● 6 peppercorns ● 2 cloves ● pinch sugar ● $\frac{1}{2}$ cup large, juicy white grapes peeled and seeded carefully ● salt

Garnish: grapes

Serve with 4 slices of bread fried in butter.

Suggested wines

Pommard, Brunello di Montalcino, Chianti

Suggested menu

Tuna and pickled pepper canapés
▷ Partridges in chocolate sauce
Rosy pears

1 Sprinkle a pinch of salt into the cavity of each bird and truss with kitchen string. Heat the oil with the bay leaf, and brown the partridges evenly. Remove birds.

2 Sauté the garlic and cloves briefly in the oil and when they have barely colored add the vinegar, wine, stock, peppercorns, and a pinch of sugar.

3 Cover and cook for 5 minutes; return the partridges to the pan and continue cooking with the lid on over low heat for 50 minutes.

4 Remove the partridges from the pan; untie the kitchen string and transfer to a heated earthenware dish. Reserve the cooking juices from the pan. Melt the chocolate with 3 tablespoons water in the top of a double boiler over hot water. Stir in the strained cooking juices. Carefully return the birds to the pan and pour in the chocolate mixture.

5 Cook over very low heat for another 15 minutes. About 5 minutes before serving add the grapes, reserving a few for decoration.

6 Place each partridge on a large slice of bread fried in butter; spoon the sauce over them and garnish with the reserved grapes. Serve at once.

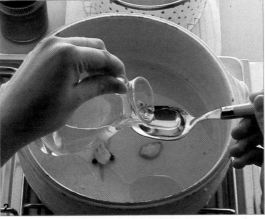

This recipe comes from Navarre in northern Spain. The delicate flavor and texture of partridge, with its low fat content, is complemented by the richness of this unusual chocolate sauce.

Stuffed roast turkey

Preparation and cooking time: 2 hours 30 minutes

Serves 6: A 5–8 lb turkey ● 2 apples ● $\frac{1}{2}$ cup ham ●
small bunch parsley ● 2 sage leaves ● 2 shallots ●
2 cups white bread, crusts removed, soaked in milk and
squeezed out ● 1 clove ● 2 eggs ● 3 tablespoons fine
breadcrumbs ● $\frac{1}{4}$ cup chicken livers ● $\frac{1}{2}$ cup butter ●
salt ● pepper

Suggested wines

Nuits-Saint-Georges, Nebbiolo, Pommard

Suggested menu

Beef consommé with sherry
▷ Stuffed roast turkey
Cinnamon pear soufflés

1 Peel, core and chop the apples; sauté them gently in half the butter.

2 Wash and trim the chicken livers; chop finely together with the ham.

3 Transfer to a bowl and add the chopped shallots, sage leaves and parsley. Add the fine breadcrumbs, eggs, the clove, sautéed chopped apple and the white bread moistened with milk; season with salt and a little freshly ground pepper.

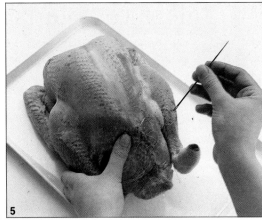

4 Mix until the ingredients are well blended. Wash and dry the turkey and season the cavity with salt and pepper; fill with the stuffing.

5 Sew up the opening and place the turkey in a roasting pan. Melt the remaining butter and spread over the breast of the turkey, sprinkle with a little salt and place in the oven, preheated to 400°F.

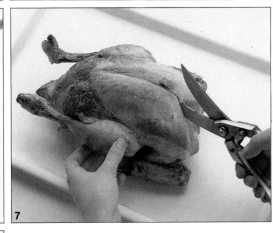

6 Halfway through the roasting time (allow about 2½–3 hours), cover the turkey with foil and continue roasting, turning the bird from time to time and basting with the juices.

7 When the turkey is done (check that the juices run clear when the thigh is pierced) remove from the oven, carve into serving pieces and serve with the stuffing and the juices from the roasting pan.

For your Thanksgiving or Christmas turkey, a more elaborate stuffing can be used. Instead of ham, use ½ lb button mushrooms; leave out the apples, shallots and sage and substitute two onions, a chopped carrot, a clove of garlic and two small, finely chopped celery stalks. The turkey liver can be used instead of the chicken livers; sauté all these ingredients, finely chopped, in butter and when they are just done, add 2 tablespoons brandy, allow to evaporate and remove from heat. Mix with the eggs, soaked white bread, chopped parsley and a little salt and pepper and then stuff the turkey as above.

Turkey à la King

Preparation and cooking time: 1 hour 25 minutes

Serves 4: 1¾ lb turkey breast (skin removed) •
1 medium-sized onion • ½ cup butter • 3 cups button
mushrooms • 1 celery stalk • 2 sweet red peppers •
1 bay leaf • 1 clove • ½ cup cream • 2 egg yolks •
1 cup dry white wine • ½ cup flour • 4 teaspoons
coarse salt • 2 peppercorns

Serve with 1½ cups pilaf rice (see recipe, p. 176)

Suggested wines

Marqués de Cacéres, Griottes Chambertin,
Cabernet Vicentino

Suggested menu

Cream of lettuce soup
▷ Turkey à la King
Orange cream

1 Slice the onion and place in saucepan with the celery, bay leaf, clove, peppercorns and salt.

2 Place the turkey breast on top of the vegetables and cover with the wine mixed with 1 pint of water. Bring to a boil and then simmer very gently for 45 minutes.

3 Allow the turkey breast to cool to room temperature in the cooking liquid; drain, dice and set aside. Discard the celery and bay leaf. Reserve stock and onions.

4 Wash and dry the mushrooms and cut into thin slices; sauté for 15 minutes in $\frac{1}{4}$ cup butter, stirring frequently then add to the reserved stock containing the onions.

5 Wash and dry peppers. Place under the broiler or hold over a gas burner to scorch the thin outer skin. Peel off the burned skin, remove the stalk, cut open and trim off the pith, removing the seeds. Cut into thin strips and add to the stock.

6 Reserve a little stock to mix with the beaten egg yolks. Melt the remaining butter in a small saucepan, stir in the flour and cook until the roux turns a pale golden brown. Add a little of the stock to dilute, then gradually stir into the stock containing the onions, mushrooms and sweet peppers. Cook for 15 minutes, stirring constantly and then mix in the cream. After a few minutes reduce the heat (or turn off) and trickle in the egg yolks, beaten with a little of the reserved stock.

7 Mix well and stir in the diced turkey. Arrange the pilaf rice on a hot serving platter and spoon the turkey and sauce on top.

"Galantine" of turkey

Preparation and cooking time: 3 hours (+ at least 4 hours for the "galantine" to set)

Serves 8: a 5–8 lb turkey • 1¼ cups Marsala • a ¼ lb slice of ham • a ¼ lb slice of pickled or pressed tongue • 4 ¼ lb slices pork fat • ¼ cup whole, shelled pistachio nuts • 1 small black truffle (canned if fresh is not available) • ¾ lb lean veal • 1 onion • 1 carrot • 1 clove • 2 calf's feet • nutmeg • coarse and fine salt • pepper

Suggested wines

Frascati, Muscadet, Bordeaux blanc

Suggested menu

▷ "Galantine" of turkey
Salmon roll
Lemon chiffon

1 Place the turkey, breast downwards, on a carving board. Cut through the neck about two inches below the bird's head and use a very sharp knife to cut through the skin all the way down the backbone.

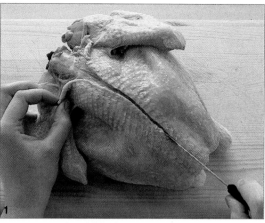

2 Gradually work the skin away from the flesh, working from first one side and then the other. Free as much of the skin on the wings as possible and then do likewise with the legs. The skin should be removed in one piece.

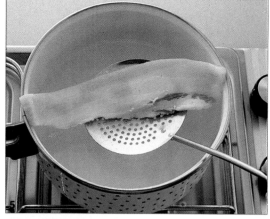

3 Roll up the skin and place in a large bowl; pour over the Marsala and leave to stand while preparing the "galantine".

4 Remove the breast from the turkey and dice evenly. Likewise dice the slices of ham and tongue.

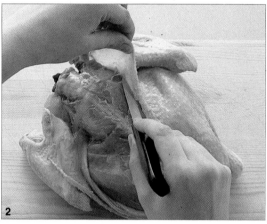

5 Blanch a slice of pork fat by placing it in a saucepan full of boiling water, reducing the heat and simmering very gently for 20 minutes. Refresh the pork fat under cold water, dry and dice finely; mix with the other diced meats.

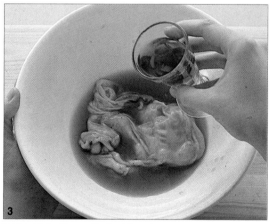

6 Season the mixture with a pinch of salt, a little freshly ground pepper and a pinch of grated nutmeg; add the pistachio nuts (blanched for a few minutes in boiling water, drained and peeled) and the peeled and thinly sliced truffle.

7 Add to the bowl containing the turkey skin and Marsala and mix. Cover and leave to stand.

8 Place the veal, the remaining unblanched pork fat and the rest of the turkey meat taken off the carcass in a food processor and blend (or put through a grinder twice).

9 Remove the rolled up turkey skin from the bowl containing the Marsala mixture and set aside; add the ground meats to the diced meats, truffle and pistachios and blend well.

10 Spread out the turkey skin very carefully and set the meat mixture on top. Shape into a long loaf.

11 Enclose the meat mixture in the skin and sew the edges securely together. Prick lightly all over with a fork.

12 Wrap the loaf in a clean white cloth, twisting and tying the ends like a candy wrapper. Tie with string to secure.

13 Place in a large pot, pour in enough water to cover and add an onion stuck with a clove, a peeled carrot, the neck of the turkey and the broken up carcass, the calf's feet (washed and slit lengthwise) and a teaspoon of coarse salt. Cook over moderate heat, removing any scum that collects on top. As soon as the water comes to a boil, turn down the heat and simmer very slowly for 1½ hours.

14 Remove the loaf carefully from the cooking liquid and place on a flat surface to cool. Remove the cloth carefully.

15 Rinse the cloth in cold water, wring out and lay flat. Wrap the loaf again and tie up as before.

16 Flatten the wrapped "galantine" by weighing it down on each end on a large plate. Do not place under too much pressure or it will lose too much moisture. Leave for at least 4 hours before serving. The "galantine" may then be sliced with a very sharp knife. Serve with chopped aspic (optional).

118

Fish and seafood

Lobster à la française

Preparation and cooking time: About 2 hours

Serves 6: 3 large cooked lobsters ● 2 pints good quality dry white wine ● ½ cup Cognac ● a bouquet garni (a few sprigs parsley, 1 bay leaf, thyme) ● 3 medium-sized onions ● 3 large shallots ● 1 clove garlic ● ¾ cup ham, diced ● 4 large tomatoes ● 1¾ cups fish stock or fumet (see recipes, p. 175) ● ¼ cup butter ● ¼ cup flour ● 1 cup oil ● salt ● pepper ● cayenne pepper

Suggested wines

Champagne brut, Spumante Oltrepò, Vernaccia di San Gimignano

Suggested menu

Tuna and pickled pepper canapés
▷ Lobster à la française
Strawberry meringues with Melba sauce

1 Cut off the tails of the lobsters as shown: remove and reserve the corals. Split the heads in half and reserve the liver (the greenish creamy substance).

2 Heat half the oil in a deep skillet and sauté the shelled tail pieces lightly; pour the Cognac over them and flame. When the flames have died down, pour in the white wine and simmer gently.

3 Chop the onions, shallots and garlic very finely and fry gently in the remaining oil for about 10 minutes; add the blanched, skinned, seeded and coarsely chopped tomatoes.

4 Stir in the diced ham and add the bouquet garni; cook over low heat, stirring occasionally, for 10 minutes.

5 Pour the tomato and ham sauce over the sautéed lobster pieces, season with salt, a little freshly ground pepper and a pinch of cayenne pepper; stir in 1¾ cups of the strained fish stock.

6 Cover and simmer gently for 20 minutes; transfer the lobster pieces to a heated serving dish, cover with foil and keep warm over hot water.

7 Remove the bouquet garni, turn up the heat and reduce the sauce by boiling, uncovered, for about 10 minutes. Blend together half the butter with the flour, coral and liver. Lower the heat and stir the mixture into the sauce.

8 Stir the sauce for a few more minutes until it thickens; add the remaining butter in small pieces. When this has been incorporated into the sauce, pour over the lobster and serve at once.

Creole scampi

Preparation and cooking time: 1 hour 10 minutes

Serves 4: 2¾ lb fresh scampi or Dublin Bay prawns •
1 medium-sized onion • 1 sweet red pepper • 1 clove
garlic • ½ cup olive oil • 1¾–2 cups button mushrooms
• 4 tomatoes • ½ cup dry white wine • half a lemon •
1 bay leaf • small bunch parsley • pinch paprika • salt
• pepper

Suggested wines

Bordeaux blanc, Pinot di Franciacorta, Muscadet

Suggested menu

▷ Creole scampi
Coffee flavored ratafia cream

1 Chop the onion and garlic finely with the parsley and sauté in the oil in a large skillet.

2 Peel the scampi and remove the black substance from the backs. Add them to the onion, garlic and parsley and sauté lightly, seasoning with a pinch of salt, pepper and paprika; pour in the white wine and cook until it has almost completely evaporated.

3 Take up the scampi, cover with foil and keep warm.

4 Wash and seed the pepper, cut into strips and add to the sauce. Stir, add the bay leaf and season with a little salt and freshly ground pepper.

5 Cook over moderate heat for 10 minutes. Trim, wash and thinly slice the mushrooms, then sprinkle with the juice of half a lemon; stir into the sauce and cook for a further 10 minutes before adding the crushed tomatoes.

6 Stir and simmer until the sauce has reduced and thickened slightly; return the warm scampi to the pan and cook for a few minutes so that they are coated with the sauce. Serve very hot.

Shellfish vol-au-vents

Preparation and cooking time: 2 hours 15 minutes

Serves 4: 8 jumbo shrimp or scampi • 8 mushrooms • ½ carrot • ½ onion • 1 shallot • 1 clove garlic • scant ½ cup butter • 3 tablespoons oil • 1¾ cups dry white wine • 1 pint fish stock (*see recipe, p. 175*) • 3 tablespoons roughly chopped tomatoes (no seeds or skin) • ½ cup cream • 1 tablespoon flour • salt • pepper

For the puff pastry: 2¼ cups butter • 4½ cups all-purpose flour • salt • cold water, as required • 1 egg

For the vol-au-vents: see method opposite or use frozen vol-au-vent cases.

Suggested wines

Pinot di Franciacorta, Chablis, Sauvignon del Collio

Suggested menu

▷ Shellfish vol-au-vents
Potato and cauliflower gratin
Almond ice cream with chocolate rum sauce

1 Sieve 3½ cups flour into a bowl, add a pinch of salt and gradually work in just enough water to give a smooth, elastic dough. Knead lightly. Wrap the dough in a damp cloth and refrigerate for 20 minutes. Work the remaining flour and the butter together, shape into a flat block; refrigerate.

2 After 20 minutes remove the flour and water dough. Roll out into a rectangle. Place butter block in center and enclose in the dough.

3 Roll out into a rectangle, fold into three and replace in the refrigerator for 10 minutes. Repeat 3 times.

4 Pull heads off shrimp. Prepare all vegetables except mushrooms, slice and sauté in 1½ tablespoons of oil and ¼ cup of butter for 10 minutes with the shrimp heads. Season, pour in just under 1 cup wine and cook until the wine has evaporated. Discard the heads.

5 Heat 2 tablespoons of the butter and the remaining oil in a separate skillet and sauté the unpeeled shrimp with the quartered mushrooms for 10 minutes. Season, add remaining wine and cook until it evaporates.

6 Sieve the vegetables; return to pan. Add 2 tablespoons of butter, worked with the flour into a *beurre manié*; stir until thick then add the tomatoes. Add the hot fish stock a little at a time. Pour in the cream and simmer for 10 minutes.

7 Take up the shrimp, discard shells and chop. Add with the mushrooms to the sauce; simmer for a few minutes. Fill each vol-au-vent case. Heat at 400°F for 5–6 minutes.

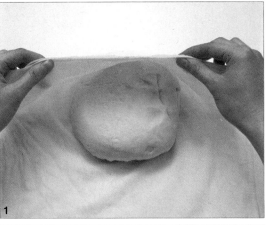

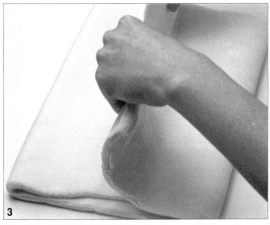

To prepare the vol-au-vent cases: Having prepared the pastry (steps 1–3) roll out to ½ inch thick and cut out circles with a 2 in fluted pastry cutter. Rinse a cookie sheet with cold water and place the circles of pastry on it. Brush the pastry with beaten egg. Using a ¾ in unfluted pastry cutter, press gently down on each circle of pastry and cut into about half the thickness of the pastry. Place the vol-au-vents in the bottom of a hot oven (450°F) and bake for about 12 minutes. Remove from the oven when the pastry has risen and is golden brown. Remove the lid and soft dough in the center to leave an opening for the filling.

125

Stuffed crab

Preparation and cooking time: 2 hours 15 minutes

Serves 4: 4 freshly killed crabs ● $\frac{1}{2}$ carrot ● $\frac{1}{2}$ onion ●
4 fresh mushrooms ● 2 cloves garlic ● 3 sprigs parsley
● $\frac{3}{4}$ cup butter ● 1 cup dry white wine ● $1\frac{3}{4}$ cups fish
stock or fumet (see recipe, p.175) ● 3 tablespoons
tomato paste ● $\frac{1}{2}$ cup cream ● 1 cup rice ●
3 tablespoons oil ● 2 shallots ● salt ● pepper ●
Hollandaise sauce (see recipe, p.175).

Suggested wines

Cortese di Gavi, Bordeaux blanc, Muscadet

Suggested menu

Vegetarian "caviar"
▷ Stuffed crab
Strawberry meringues with Melba sauce

1 Heat just under half the butter in a large skillet and cook the crabs for about 30 minutes over moderate heat, turning several times, until they are a dull red color and are cooked through.

2 Leave to cool. Remove the large claws and set aside. Twist off the small claws. Turn the crab upside down and remove the pointed flap.

3 Pull the two halves of the crab apart and reserve the top part. Discard the greyish stomach-sac but retain the coral. Remove all the meat from the legs and body and set aside.

4 Heat 1½ tablespoons of butter and sauté the chopped carrot and onion. Add the claws and sauté for a few minutes. Pour in the dry white wine, allow to evaporate, then add the fish stock, tomato paste, a clove of garlic and the parsley. Cook for 20 minutes over moderate heat.

5 Strain the sauce and return to the pan over gentle heat.

6 Pour in the cream and simmer until the sauce has reduced by about half. Leave to cool. Gradually whisk in the Hollandaise sauce.

7 Boil the rice. Chop the shallots and fry gently in the oil and 2 tablespoons of butter. Add the rice and sauté for a few minutes.

8 Slice the mushrooms. Sauté in 3 tablespoons of butter with the remaining garlic and season. Fill each crab shell with alternating layers of rice, mushrooms and crab meat, and top with sauce. Place on a cookie sheet and place in the oven, preheated to 475°F for 15 minutes.

Shrimp and mushroom crêpes

Preparation and cooking time: 1 hour

Serves 4: 16 crêpes (see recipe, p. 160)

For the filling: 1 cup shelled shrimp ● 1 celery stalk ● 1 cup mushrooms or a packet dried Italian porcini mushrooms, soaked in warm water for 15–20 minutes ● $\frac{1}{2}$ onion ● 1 clove garlic ● pinch of grated nutmeg ● 2 sage leaves ● 5 tablespoons olive oil ● $\frac{1}{3}$ cup fresh breadcrumbs ● 5 tablespoons cream ● 1 teaspoon lemon juice ● $\frac{1}{2}$ cup dry vermouth ● 1 egg yolk ● salt ● pepper

For the sauce: 3 tablespoons butter ● $\frac{1}{4}$ cup + 3 tablespoons flour ● 1 pint light stock ● $\frac{1}{2}$ cup dry white wine ● 1 egg yolk ● 1 tablespoon tomato paste ● salt ● white pepper ● 5 tablespoons grated Parmesan cheese ● $1\frac{1}{2}$ tablespoons butter

Suggested wines

Riesling Napa Valley, Cortese di Gavi, Bordeaux blanc

Suggested menu

▷ Shrimp and mushroom crêpes
Rainbow salad
Iced melon cream

128

1 Prepare the crêpes as directed in the recipe on page 160.
To prepare the filling: Chop the onion, garlic clove and celery finely and fry gently in the oil until soft.

2 Add the shelled shrimp and sauté for 5 minutes if raw (if cooked, warm through for about a minute); add the washed and chopped mushrooms. Add a little salt and freshly ground pepper, a pinch of grated nutmeg and two chopped sage leaves. Simmer for 10 minutes and then sprinkle in the lemon juice and the breadcrumbs; stir in the vermouth and then the cream and egg yolk.

3 Place equal amounts of this filling on each crêpe and roll up.

4 *To prepare the sauce*: Melt the butter in a saucepan, stir in the flour and gradually add the hot stock, stirring constantly to prevent any lumps. Gradually add the dry white wine and season with salt and white pepper. Remove from the heat and whisk in the beaten egg yolk in a thin stream. Stir in the tomato paste.

5 Place the rolled up crêpes in a shallow ovenproof dish and coat evenly with the sauce.

6 Sprinkle with 5 tablespoons grated Parmesan cheese and dot with butter. Place in a preheated oven at 350°F for 25 minutes until the top is lightly browned.

Deep-fried oysters

Preparation and cooking time: 50 minutes

Serves 4: 24 cleaned, shucked oysters ● ¾ cup milk ●
oil for deep-frying ● 6 tablespoons flour ● 2 eggs ●
1 cup fine breadcrumbs ● salt ● pepper

Garnish: lemon wedges, shredded lettuce and fresh
parsley

Suggested wines

Chardonnay Napa Valley, Cortese di Gavi,
Bordeaux blanc

Suggested menu

▷ Deep-fried oysters
Roast veal with mixed herbs
Strawberries with sherry

1 Rinse the oysters in cold water and drain well.

2 Place the oysters in a bowl and cover with the milk; leave to stand for 15 minutes.

3 Drain the oysters thoroughly and turn onto paper towels; pat dry all over.

4 Season with a little salt and freshly ground pepper.

5 Roll the oysters in the flour, coating each one thoroughly.

6 Beat the eggs in a bowl with a little salt and pepper and dip each oyster into this mixture.

7 Coat the oysters in the breadcrumbs, pressing the crumbs to adhere firmly to the oyster.

8 Heat the oil in a deep skillet or a wok; when the oil is very hot lower the oysters in carefully and fry until golden brown. Drain well and serve at once, garnished with lemon wedges, shredded lettuce and fresh parsley.

Oysters Florentine

Suggested wines

Bianco Val di Chiana, Volnay, Chablis

Suggested menu

Vegetarian "Caviar"
▷ Oysters Florentine
Rosy pears

Preparation and cooking time: 1 hour

Serves 4: 24 fresh oysters ● 14 oz lightly boiled fresh spinach (or use frozen) ● 1 large shallot ● ¾ cup dry white wine ● 1¾ cups fish stock (see recipe, p. 175) ● ¼ cup butter ● ¼ cup flour ● 1 cup cream ● 2 egg yolks ● 1 teaspoon oil ● 1 teaspoon lemon juice ● salt ● white pepper

1 Scrub the shells and with an oyster knife or other very strong knife, prise the shell open and remove the oyster.

2 Pour the liquor from the shells through a fine sieve into a bowl.

3 Chop the shallot finely and sauté in half the butter until pale golden brown. Add the oysters and the dry white wine and simmer, stirring and turning gently, for 2–3 minutes. Season with a little salt and freshly ground white pepper. Remove the oysters with a slotted spoon and keep warm.

4 Melt the remaining butter in another pan. Stir in the flour and gradually mix in the hot fish stock. Stir until the sauce has thickened and then add the oyster liquor, the lemon juice and a little more salt if necesssary. Finally, beat the egg yolks with the cream and gradually stir into the sauce. Remove from heat.

5 Rinse the spinach very well and heat gently for 5 minutes with no added water and with a pinch of salt. Refresh under cold water, chop coarsely and warm in the wine and juices left over from cooking the oysters.

6 Place the carefully cleaned oyster shells on a lightly greased cookie sheet and fill each shell with spinach; top with an oyster. Coat with a spoonful of sauce and bake in a preheated oven at 400°F for 20 minutes.

Squid española

Preparation and cooking time: 1 hour 15 minutes

Serves 4: 4 large or 8 small squid ● $\frac{1}{2}$ cup diced ham ●
1 cup red wine ● $\frac{1}{4}$ cup diced salt pork (or smoked
pancetta) ● 2 green peppers ● 1 bay leaf ● 2 leeks ●
1 onion ● 1 clove garlic ● $\frac{2}{3}$ cup oil ● $1\frac{1}{2}$ cups stock ●
3 tablespoons tomato paste ● generous pinch paprika
● salt ● pepper

Suggested wines

Soave, Bordeaux blanc, Vernaccia di San
Gimignano

Suggested menu

Brain and herb soup
▷ Squid española
Lemon chiffon

1 Pull the head and tentacles away from the body together with the thin transparent "pen". Rub off the purple outer skin under warm water; wash the body in cold water and pat dry. Chop the tentacles, discarding the head and "pen."

2 Cut off and chop the triangular fins and mix with the chopped tentacles, the diced ham and 3 tablespoons of oil, a pinch of salt and a little freshly ground pepper.

3 Stuff the squid with this mixture, securing the opening with a toothpick.

4 Heat 6 tablespoons oil in a skillet; place the stuffed squid in the pan and fry until golden brown on both sides. When they are tender, season with salt and a little freshly ground pepper.

5 Blanch the diced salt pork in boiling water for a few minutes and drain well.

6 Peel the onion; trim and wash the leeks; slice into thin rings. Fry gently in 6 tablespoons oil with the finely chopped garlic.

7 Add the red wine to this mixture and cook over high heat until the wine has almost completely evaporated; stir occasionally to prevent the vegetables from sticking. Stir in the tomato paste, stock, diced salt pork, bay leaf, chopped green peppers, and season with a pinch of salt and paprika. Cook briskly for 15 minutes, allowing the sauce to reduce. Turn down the heat, add the fried stuffed squid and simmer for 10 minutes more. Transfer to a heated serving dish and serve piping hot.

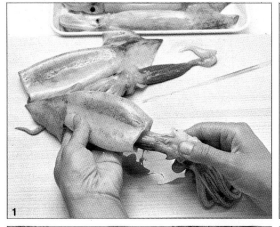

Stuffed squid

Preparation and cooking time: 1 hour 30 minutes

Serves 4: 1 $1\frac{1}{4}$–$1\frac{1}{2}$ lb squid ● 5 oz fillet of sole ● 1 egg ● 1 egg yolk ● $\frac{3}{4}$ cup cream ● 2 carrots ● $1\frac{1}{4}$–$1\frac{1}{2}$ lb fresh green beans ● $\frac{1}{2}$ sweet red pepper ● $\frac{1}{4}$ onion ● 1 pint dry white wine ● salt ● pepper

For the sauce: 1 cup mayonnaise ● $\frac{1}{4}$ teaspoon grated horseradish ● 3 tablespoons ketchup ● 6 tablespoons cream ● 1 tablespoon lemon juice

Garnish: watercress

Suggested wines

Muscadet, Bourgogne blanc, Cortese di Gavi

Suggested menu

Ham, egg and cheese risotto
▷ Stuffed squid
Caramelized pears

1 Pull the head and tentacles away from the body of the squid and remove the thin transparent spine. Rub off the dark outer skin under warm water (or pull off); wash in cold water and pat dry. Cut tentacles from head.

2 Chop the sole fillet with a very sharp knife and add the tentacles if desired.

3 Using a mortar and pestle, reduce the sole to a smooth paste and blend together with the whole egg and the egg yolk. (Alternatively, use an electric blender or food processor.) Stir in the cream seasoned with a little salt and freshly ground pepper.

4 Cut the pepper and a carrot into long strips; blanch the green beans in a little salted water for a few minutes. Spoon about half the sole and egg mixture into the squid, followed by the strips of pepper, carrot and beans. Fill up with the remaining sole and egg mixture.

5 Sew up the end of the squid.

6 Pour the wine into a large saucepan, add 1 pint of water and the remaining peeled and chopped carrot, the sliced onion and a little salt and pepper. Place the stuffed squid in this cooking liquid and simmer for 45 minutes, turning occasionally.

7 *To prepare the sauce*: Whisk the ketchup into the mayonnaise and then add the cream, grated horseradish and lemon juice. When the squid is cooked, drain and cut carefully into slices with a very sharp knife and cover with some of the sauce. Garnish with watercress and serve the remaining sauce separately.

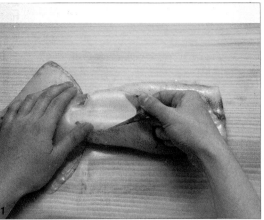

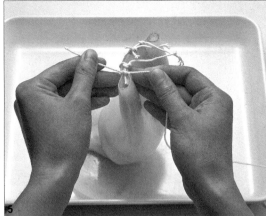

If very large squid are not available, prepare four smaller ones, one per person, in which case a little more stuffing may be needed.

137

San Sebastian sea bream

Preparation and cooking time: 40 minutes (+ 1 hour for marinating the fish)

Serves 4: 1 2¼ lb sea bream ● 4 cloves garlic ● 2–3 tablespoons finely chopped parsley ● small piece red chili pepper ● juice of 1 large lemon ● ⅔ cup oil ● salt ● pepper

Suggested wines

Cortese di Gavi, Muscadet, Lugana

Suggested menu

Green risotto with mixed herbs
▷ San Sebastian sea bream
Melon filled with fruit salad

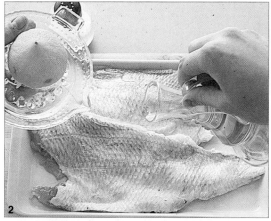

1 Cut the fish in half and carefully remove the backbone; wash the fish and pat dry with paper towels. Place the two halves flat in a dish.

2 Sprinkle the fish with a pinch of salt, 3 tablespoons of lemon juice and 3 tablespoons of oil; cover and leave to marinate for about 1 hour in a cool place.

3 Broil the fish, basting frequently with 2–3 tablespoons of oil and turning several times so that it cooks evenly.

4 Heat the remaining oil in a small saucepan together with the garlic cloves and the piece of chili pepper, then add a pinch of salt and 3 tablespoons lemon juice.

5 Carefully transfer the fish from the broiler to a heated serving plate.

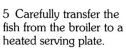

6 Sprinkle with the chopped parsley and the garlic- and chili-flavored oil (discard solids). Serve very hot.

Hake with tomato and mustard sauce

Preparation and cooking time: 1 hour

Serves 4: 2 large hake fillets ● 4 large ripe tomatoes ● 3 tablespoons Dijon mustard ● 1 tablespoon fine breadcrumbs ● 1 cup dry white wine ● 4 large mushrooms ● 2 tablespoons butter ● salt ● pepper

Suggested wines

Muscadet, Bourgogne blanc, Cortese di Gavi

Suggested menu

Cream of asparagus soup with chervil and ham
▷ Hake with tomato and mustard sauce
Orange frost

1 Season the hake fillets with a little salt and pepper.

2 Blanch the tomatoes. Remove skin and seeds; chop coarsely. Butter an ovenproof dish and spoon the chopped tomatoes around the side.

3 Place the hake fillets in the center of the dish.

4 Spread the mustard evenly over the hake fillets.

5 Sprinkle the fish with fine breadcrumbs and then pour in the white wine.

6 Place the dish on a cookie sheet and bake for 30 minutes at 350°F. When the fish is cooked, arrange the washed, dried and thinly sliced raw or blanched mushrooms on top. Serve at once.

Fried hake *maître d'hôtel*

Preparation and cooking time: 40 minutes (+ 2 hours for the *maître d'hôtel* butter to chill)

Serves 4: 8 small hake ● 2 eggs ● all-purpose flour for coating fish ● 2 cups fine breadcrumbs ● 6 tablespoons white wine vinegar ● oil for frying ● salt ● pepper

For the maître d'hôtel *butter*: ½ cup butter, juice of half a lemon ● 1–2 tablespoons finely chopped parsley

Garnish: parsley

Serve with steamed potatoes

Suggested wines

Muscadet, Soave, Bordeaux blanc

Suggested menu

Lettuce and ham risotto
▷ Fried hake *maître d'hôtel*
Blancmange

142

1 Work the butter until soft and then mix in the chopped parsley, followed by the lemon juice.

2 Roll the butter into a fat "sausage" in wax paper or foil (about 1¼ in in diameter). Chill in the refrigerator for at least 2 hours.

3 Gut the fish, wash well and dry.

4 Pour the vinegar into a bowl and dilute with an equal amount of cold water. Use a clean cloth wrapped around three fingers and dipped in this acidulated water to wipe the cavities of the fish; do not rinse off.

5 Coat the fish in flour and dip into the egg beaten with a little salt.

6 Roll in the breadcrumbs, pressing lightly so that the whole fish is coated.

7 Heat plenty of oil until very hot in a large skillet and lower the fish carefully into the pan.

8 Fry the fish until they are well browned, spooning hot oil over them occasionally. Remove and drain on paper towels. Slice the *maître d'hôtel* butter and place a round of butter on each fish. Garnish with sprigs of parsley and serve with steamed potatoes.

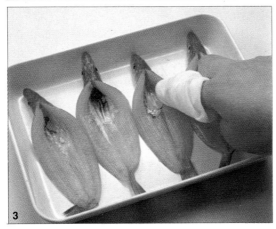

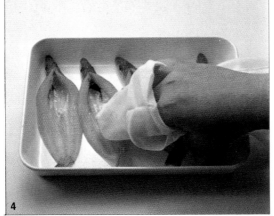

Fillets of turbot in champagne sauce

Preparation and cooking time: About 1 hour

Serves 4: 4 fillets of turbot • 2 finely chopped shallots • 6 tablespoons butter • 3 tablespoons flour • 1 cup fish stock or fumet (*see recipe, p. 175*) • 6 tablespoons cream • 1¼ cups button mushrooms • ¾ cup dry champagne • 2 egg yolks • salt • pepper

Suggested wines

Bordeaux blanc, Cortese di Gavi, Greco di Tufo

Suggested menu

Penne with radicchio
▷ Fillets of turbot in champagne sauce
Lemon chiffon

1 Trim the mushrooms, wash, dry and slice thinly.

2 Heat $\frac{1}{4}$ cup of butter and gently sauté the chopped shallots until pale golden brown; add the mushrooms and the turbot fillets (make sure all skin and bones have been removed).

3 Add a pinch of salt and a little freshly ground pepper, pour in the champagne and a few spoonfuls of fish stock and simmer very gently for 20 minutes, turning the fish fillets carefully halfway through cooking time.

4 Remove the turbot fillets and place in an ovenproof dish, cover with the mushrooms and a sheet of foil and keep warm.

5 Melt the remaining butter in a small saucepan; stir in the flour quickly and thoroughly to avoid lumps. Gradually add the remaining fish stock.

6 Continue cooking until the stock is used up and stir over low heat until the sauce has thickened. Season with a little salt and freshly ground pepper.

7 Stir in the egg yolks, beaten with the cream. Remove from heat.

8 Pour this sauce over the fish and mushrooms and place, uncovered, in the oven, preheated to 350°F, for a few minutes to lightly brown the top. Serve at once.

Sea bass en croûte

Preparation and cooking time: 1 hour 30 minutes

Serves 4: A fillet of sea bass about 12 in long ● 10 thin slices smoked salmon ● 2 tablespoons butter ● large packet frozen puff pastry

For the stuffing: ½ lb mushrooms (dried porcini, if available) ● 3 tablespoons finely chopped onion ● scant 1 cup cream ● 1 teaspoon flour ● 2 tablespoons butter ● salt ● white pepper

Glaze for the pastry: 1 egg yolk beaten with 1 teaspoon water and a pinch of salt (retain egg white)

Serve with Hollandaise sauce (see recipe, p. 175).

Suggested wines

Soave, Muscadet, Bordeaux blanc

Suggested menu

Poached eggs with tarragon sauce Aurore
▷ Sea bass en croûte
Cherry charlotte

1 Lay the sea bream fillet flat and season with salt and a little freshly ground pepper

2 Brown the fish briskly on both sides in 2 tablespoons of butter, take up and set aside.

3 Wash and chop the mushrooms, mix with the chopped onion and sauté in 2 tablespoons of butter.

4 Season the mushrooms with salt and white pepper, stir in the flour, followed by the cream and cook over moderate heat for 10 minutes. Remove from heat and allow to cool.

5 Having allowed the frozen pastry to thaw completely, roll out into two thin sheets. Place one sheet on a lightly buttered cookie sheet and place the fish on top. Cut around the fish, leaving a border of at least ¾ in.

6 Press the mushroom and onion mixture over the top of the fillet.

7 Cover with the smoked salmon slices, placed diagonally across the fillet.

8 Cover with the other sheet of dough and trim into a fish shape. Brush the inside edges of the pastry case with the egg white and press firmly together to seal. Make a few small diagonal incisions across the top of the pastry case to allow steam to escape during cooking and cut out decorative shapes from the remaining pastry for the eyes, scales and fins. Brush the surface with the egg glaze and bake in a preheated oven at 350°F for 30 minutes. While the fish is baking, make the hollandaise sauce (see recipe, p. 175) which should be served separately.

Tricolor roulades of sole

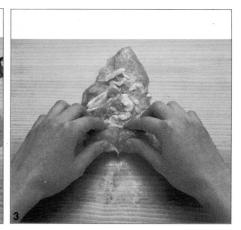

Preparation and cooking time: 1 hour 30 minutes

Serves 4: 2 whole sole • 1 cup crab meat • 1 cup shelled shrimp or scampi, finely chopped • 1 shallot • 1 pint fish stock (*see recipe*, p. 175) • 1 cup dry white wine • 1 cup cream • ½ lb finely chopped cooked spinach • 1 tablespoon lemon juice • ¼ cup butter • 2 tablespoons fine breadcrumbs • 4 large firm salad tomatoes • salt • pepper

Suggested wines

Rosé de Provence, Chiaretto del Garda, Beaujolais Villages

Suggested menu

Ham and walnut risotto
▷ Tricolor roulades of sole
Moist date cake

1 Place the sole flat on the working surface and pull off the skin from both sides: to do this make a shallow cut across the skin just below the head and pull towards the tail.

2 Use a very sharp pointed knife to fillet the fish, working the flesh carefully away from the bones.

3 Season each fillet with a pinch of salt and freshly ground pepper and spread each one with the mixed crab and shrimp meat; roll up and fasten with a small steel skewer or toothpick.

4 Melt 2 tablespoons of butter in a small saucepan, pour in the fish stock, the dry white wine

and the chopped shallot and bring to a gentle boil. Add the rolled sole fillets, cover with a sheet of foil and simmer gently for 15 minutes. Take up the fish roulades and keep warm.

5 Pour the cream into the cooking liquid and add the finely chopped or sieved spinach and lemon juice; stir to blend well.

6 Slice tomatoes in half and place on a buttered cookie sheet. Sprinkle with breadcrumbs and salt. Top with a few flakes of butter and bake in the oven at 350°F for 15 minutes. Pour the green sauce onto a shallow heated serving plate; arrange the tomatoes in the center, each topped with half a sole roulade.

Stuffed trout with almonds

Preparation and cooking time: 1 hour 15 minutes

Serves 4: 4 boned whole trout • 2 eggs • 1 cup soft breadcrumbs • a little milk • 2 onions • 2 scallions or shallots • 1 cup dry white wine • 1 tablespoon butter • a few tablespoons fine breadcrumbs • $\frac{1}{2}$ cup slivered almonds • $\frac{1}{2}$ cup oil • salt • pepper

Suggested wines

Bordaux blanc, Greco di Tufo, Frascati

Suggested menu

Green risotto with mixed herbs
▷ Stuffed trout with almonds
Caramelized apricots

150

1 Hard-boil an egg, place under cold running water, remove the shell and mash with a fork. Moisten the soft breadcrumbs with a little milk, squeeze well and then mix with the mashed hard-boiled egg.

2 Sauté the finely chopped onion and scallions or shallots gently in 3 tablespoons of oil, season with salt and pepper and then blend with the breadcrumb and egg mixture. Stir in the remaining egg.

3 Fill the cavity of each trout with a quarter of this stuffing.

4 Sew up the sides of the trout or secure with toothpicks.

5 Brush the trout with oil and coat with fine breadcrumbs.

6 Arrange the trout in a lightly greased ovenproof dish and pour in the white wine.

7 Sprinkle the slivered almonds over the fish.

8 Grease a piece of foil and place on top of the trout, buttered side down. Bake in a preheated oven (350°F) for about 30 minutes, spooning some of the wine and cooking juices over the fish occasionally to keep moist. Remove the foil after twenty minutes to allow almonds to brown. Serve immediately.

Salmon mousse

Preparation and cooking time: 45 minutes (+ 2 hours for the mousse to set)

Serves 4: 3 ½ lb/250 g can salmon • 5 oz sliced smoked salmon • scant cup thick homemade mayonnaise (see recipe, p. 175) • 1⅓ cup whipping cream • juice of 1 lemon • 3 leaves gelatine (if not available use powdered gelatine, 1 packet should suffice) • 1 teaspoon sweet almond oil • salt • pepper

Serve with slices of toast and curls of fresh, unsalted butter and diced fish aspic (see recipe, p. 175)

Suggested wines

Traminer Alto Adige, Chablis, Sauvignon del Collio

Suggested menu

▷ Salmon mousse
Savory turkey rolls
Strawberry meringues with Melba sauce

1 Soak the leaf gelatine for 30 minutes in ½ cup of cold water. If powdered gelatine is used, follow the directions on the packet.

2 Drain the canned salmon and discard any pieces of bone and skin. Chop the smoked salmon coarsely and add both to the mayonnaise in a blender or food processor. Process until the mixture is very smooth and creamy.

3 Whip the chilled cream (keeping it in the refrigerator until the last possible moment). When thick, fold in gradually to the salmon mixture.

4 Add the strained lemon juice a few drops at a time. Season with salt (if needed) and a little freshly ground white pepper.

5 Slowly melt the softened leaf gelatine in the top of a double boiler, having first squeezed free as much moisture as possible. Alternatively, follow the instructions on the packet of powdered gelatine. Pour in a thin stream into the mousse, whisking vigorously; beat well for about 5 minutes to make sure that the gelatine is evenly distributed and thoroughly blended.

6 Turn the salmon mousse into a mold, lightly oiled with the almond oil. Place in the refrigerator for 2 hours or leave overnight until set.

7 Just before serving, run the point of a very sharp knife around the top of the inside of the mold; immerse the mold in a bowl of very hot water for a few seconds and then turn out onto a chilled serving dish. Arrange a garnish of diced aspic all around the mold and serve well chilled with toast and butter.

Strips of smoked salmon and slices of peeled lemon can be used for extra decoration.

Rainbow terrine

Preparation and cooking time: 40 minutes (+ 3 hours to chill)

Serves 6: 14 oz sea bass fillets ● 1 cup peeled shrimp ● 1 pint cream ● 2 eggs ● 3 tablespoons lemon juice ● ¾ cup dry white wine ● nutmeg ● 5 oz fresh salmon fillets ● 1 lb fresh spinach, cooked ● 3 tablespoons finely chopped shallots ● 2 tablespoons butter ● 1 tablespoon oil ● salt ● white pepper

Suggested wines

Muscadet, Bourgogne blanc, Cortese di Gavi

Suggested menu

Cream of asparagus soup with chervil and ham
▷ Rainbow terrine
Banana almond crunch

1 Chop the sea bass fillets finely and mix with the peeled shrimp, the beaten eggs, half the dry white wine and cream and 1 tablespoon of lemon juice. Season with a little salt, pepper and nutmeg.

2 Blend this mixture in a food processor, reducing it to a smooth, creamy consistency. Transfer three-quarters of the mixture to a bowl.

3 To the mixture remaining in the food processor add the coarsely chopped fresh salmon, the remaining dry white wine, cream and 1 tablespoon lemon juice. Blend and turn into a bowl.

4 Chop spinach finely. Chop shallot finely and sauté until lightly colored in the butter; add the spinach and sauté for a minute or two. Season with salt and pepper, add remaining lemon juice and blend in the food processor. Turn into a bowl.

5 Line a greased rectangular cake pan with wax paper lightly brushed with oil. Carefully spoon a third of the palest mixture over the bottom.

6 Next, use all the spinach mixture to cover the first layer and then cover this with another third of the paler mixture. Spoon in all the salmon mixture, and top with the rest of the pale mixture.

7 Place the terrine in hot water in an ovenproof dish. Cover with foil and bake in a preheated oven at 325°F for 1 hour. Allow to cool; turn out of the cake pan and peel off the paper. Refrigerate before serving.

155

Crab in aspic

Preparation and cooking time: 1 hour 20 minutes (+ 4 hours for the aspic to set)

Serves 4: 1 lb/450 g fresh or canned crab meat ●
8 black olives ● 4 medium-sized tomatoes ●
1 cucumber ● 1 green pepper ● 1 packet powdered
gelatine ● 1 tablespoon lemon juice ● 3 tablespoons
medium-dry sherry ● 2 hard-boiled eggs ● salt

Suggested wines

Tocai del Collio, Lugana, Muscadet

Suggested menu

▷ Crab in aspic
Baked stuffed tomatoes
Peach Melba

1 Cut the tomatoes horizontally in half, remove the seeds and sprinkle with a little salt; turn upside down and leave for 20 minutes for the salt to draw out the water; pat dry and dice. Dice the cucumber, sprinkle with salt and leave to drain in a colander for 20 minutes.

2 Add the gelatine to a little cold water to soften, then dissolve in 1 pint warm water, stirring over low heat for 5 minutes (do not allow to boil). Add the lemon juice and the sherry, remove from heat and allow to cool; chill for 10 minutes in the refrigerator.

3 Spoon 6 tablespoons of the gelatine into a ring mold standing in a bowl of ice water. Brush the inside of the mold with gelatine, which should still be liquid; it will solidify and coat the surface. Place the black olives 1 in apart in the bottom of the mold; slice the hard-boiled eggs and arrange around the sides of the mold. Cover with a little more of the gelatine, allow to set and then add half the diced tomatoes; add more gelatine, allow to solidify and then arrange the diced cucumber on top.

4 Remove any pieces of bone or shell from the crab.

5 Cut the crab meat into pieces and arrange around the sides of the mold. Add the remaining diced tomatoes and then pour in the remainder of the gelatine. Chill in the refrigerator for 4 hours.

6 After chilling, dip the mold for a few seconds in a large bowl of hot water; invert onto a chilled serving plate.

Salmon and potato "Saint-Jacques"

Preparation and cooking time: 1 hour 50 minutes

Serves 4: 4 scallop shells ● 1½ cups sliced potatoes ●
6 oz fresh salmon ● 2 green chili peppers ● 2 egg yolks
● 1 tablespoon wine vinegar ● juice of 1 lemon ●
3 tablespoons soy sauce ● 2 tablespoons butter ●
6 tablespoons oil ● salt

Suggested wines

Muscadet, Frascati, Bordeaux blanc

Suggested menu

Vegetable and cheese quiche
▷ Salmon and potato "Saint-Jacques"
Pineapple rings in rum custard

1 Remove the skin and any bones from the fresh salmon and slice diagonally into thin pieces; place in a bowl with the lemon juice and soy sauce. Leave to marinate for 30 minutes; strain and reserve the marinade.

2 Peel the potatoes, slice thinly, rinse under cold water and pat dry; steam until tender in a colander over a pan of boiling water.

3 When the potatoes are done, place in a large bowl, sprinkle with salt, stir in a little butter, mash well and add the vinegar.

4 Whisk the egg yolks, adding the oil a few drops at a time while beating well, so that the oil is incorporated into the egg yolk evenly.

5 Pour this egg and oil mixture into the mashed potatoes and blend well.

6 Strain the marinade through a muslin cloth and add a little of the liquid to the potato mixture to add color and flavor.

7 Brush the scallop shells with a little oil and place a few salmon slices in each. Cover with the potato mixture and smooth the surface with a spatula dipped in water. Garnish with a few rings of green chili pepper and bake in a preheated oven at 350°F for 30 minutes. Serve piping hot.

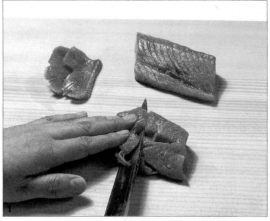

Jumbo seafood crêpes

Preparation and cooking time: 1 hour 30 minutes (+ 2 hours for the crêpe batter to stand)

Serves 4: *For the crêpes*: 1 cup all-purpose flour ●
2 eggs ● 1 pint milk ● small bunch parsley, finely
chopped ● grated rind of half an orange ●
5 tablespoons butter ● salt ● pepper

For the filling: 24 mussels ● 6 large mushrooms,
trimmed, cleaned and quartered ● 24 shrimp ●
12 scallops ● 1 onion ● 1 cup dry white wine ●
3 tablespoons butter ● *beurre manié* (a small piece
butter worked with 1 teaspoon flour) ● 1 cup cream ●
salt ● pepper

Suggested wines

Pinot d'Alsace, Riesling dell'Oltrepò Pavese, Saint-
Estèphe

Suggested menu

Brain and herb soup
▷ Seafood crêpes
Chilled peach delight

160

1 Scrub mussels and remove beards.

2 Place the sliced onion and the white wine in a large pan; add the mussels and heat until the shells open. Discard any that do not open.

3 Remove the mussels from their shells and pull off the dark-colored band that runs down the back. Reserve cooking liquid.

4 Melt 3 tablespoons of butter in a saucepan, add the uncooked shrimp, the washed scallops and the quartered mushrooms. Season. Sauté gently for a few minutes. Take up shrimp and shell.

5 Simmer the cream with the reserved cooking liquid in another heavy-bottomed skillet; stir in the *beurre manié* and season.

6 Add the mushrooms, mussels, scallops and shelled shrimp; stir and simmer for 10 minutes over moderate heat.

7 *To prepare the crêpes*: Pour the milk into an electric mixer and add the eggs, flour, a pinch of salt and a tablespoon of melted butter. Blend thoroughly until smooth. Stir in the finely chopped parsley and the grated orange rind and chill in the refrigerator for 2 hours. Melt a knob of butter in a non-stick skillet, heat until it starts to foam and then pour in a little batter in a thin layer. When the crêpe has browned underneath, turn and cook the other side. Continue until all the batter has been used up. Place about 2 tablespoons of the seafood mixture in the middle of each crêpe and gather up the edges towards the center to form a small bag and twist to secure. Serve at once.

Rice with chicken and lobster

Preparation and cooking time: 1 hour 25 minutes

Serves 4: A 2¾ lb roasting chicken ● ¾ lb fresh or canned lobster meat ● 2 bell peppers ● 2 medium-sized onions ● 4 large ripe tomatoes ● ¾ cup long-grain rice ● 1 cup oil ● 6 teaspoons soy sauce ● pepper

Suggested wines

Pinot bianco dell'Alto Adige, Pinot d'Alsace, Riesling

Suggested menu

▷ Rice with chicken and lobster
Peach and wine chiffon

1 Skin and bone the chicken and cut into strips.

2 Dice the lobster flesh (drain well if canned).

3 Pour ½ cup of oil into a large, heavy-bottomed pan and sauté the strips of chicken; add the diced lobster and continue cooking over low heat for up to 20 minutes.

4 Wash and dry the green peppers, remove the seeds and white membrane; peel the onions and chop these and the peppers coarsely. Dice the tomatoes and add to the peppers, onions and the remaining oil in another saucepan; cook over high heat for a few minutes.

5 Sprinkle the rice into the saucepan with the vegetables and continue cooking, stirring constantly, for 5 minutes more.

6 Add the rice, tomato and pepper mixture to the pan containing the pieces of chicken and lobster.

7 Add the soy sauce and plenty of freshly ground pepper; stir well and add just enough warm water to cover the rice. Boil briskly for 10 minutes, until the rice is tender but still firm. Transfer to a preheated serving dish and serve with extra soy sauce.

This is an unusual main dish with a rich oriental flavor, yet very simple to prepare.

163

Paella

Preparation and cooking time: 1 hour 30 minutes

Serves 8: A 3¼ lb chicken (cut into small pieces) ● 14 oz pork (cut into bite-sized pieces) ● 8 peeled jumbo shrimp ● 8 small spicy sausages ● 14 oz squid (cut into rings) ● 32 shelled mussels ● 8 small pieces filleted white fish ● 2⅔ cups arborio rice ● 12 artichoke hearts ● ½ cup cooked peas ● 4 sweet red peppers, cut into strips ● 1 small onion, finely chopped ● 2 cloves garlic ● 2 cups sauce tomatoes ● 5 tablespoons chopped parsley ● 2 packets saffron ● 5¼ cups light meat stock ● 1¾ cups oil ● 3 tablespoons fresh pork fat or shortening ● salt ● pepper

Suggested wines

Chiaretto del Garda, Médoc, Rosé de Provence

Suggested menu

▷ Paella
Almond ice cream with chocolate rum sauce

1 Use a special paella pan or a large cast-iron skillet for this dish. Heat just over half the oil and all the fat until very hot; fry the pieces of chicken and pork, and the squid rings.

2 Add the finely chopped onion and stir until golden brown; add the artichoke hearts.

3 When the artichoke hearts have browned add the sauce tomatoes cut into strips. Simmer for 5 minutes, add half a cup of stock and simmer for another 10 minutes. During this time the pieces of fish and the shrimp can be sautéed in another pan in a little oil and set aside.

4 Add the rice, peas and strips of sweet red pepper to the simmering tomatoes and onions; add more hot stock as needed.

5 Use a mortar and pestle to crush the garlic cloves into a paste and mix with the saffron in a little hot stock; add to the rice and other ingredients.

6 Add the sautéed pieces of fish and shrimp.

7 Add the mussels and the sausages (fried separately in 3 tablespoons oil).

8 Adjust the seasoning and place in the oven, preheated to 350°F, until all excess moisture has been absorbed (the rice should be tender but still firm). Before serving, sprinkle with finely chopped parsley.

Mediterranean fish stew

Preparation and cooking time: 1 hour 30 minutes

Serves 8: 4 medium-sized onions • scant ½ cup oil •
1 lb fish trimmings (tails, heads, bones, etc.) • 5 large
ripe tomatoes • 1 lb shellfish (fresh, preferably
uncooked) • 2–3½ lb assorted fresh fish (monkfish,
turbot, sole, mussels, hake, whiting or whatever fresh
fish is available) • ¾ cup dry white wine • 1 clove garlic
• 1 bouquet garni (bay leaf, thyme, parsley and fennel)
• 1 packet saffron threads • salt • pepper

For the accompanying sauce: 3 egg yolks • 1 clove
garlic • 1 cup good quality olive oil • salt • pepper

Serve with: toasted garlic bread sprinkled with
Parmesan and chopped parsley

Suggested wines

Rosé de Provence, Lagrein rosato, Faisca rosé

Suggested menu

▷ Mediterranean fish stew
Rainbow salad
Apples flamed in rum

1 Peel the onions, slice very thinly and heat gently in the oil in a large, heavy-bottomed pan.

2 Continue cooking, stirring frequently, until the onions are golden brown.

3 Add the fish trimmings and stir for a few minutes over fairly high heat; pour in the dry white wine, season with a little salt and freshly ground pepper and bring to a boil. Pour in enough water to completely cover and bring back to a boil.

4 Blanch, peel and remove the seeds from the tomatoes; chop coarsely and add to the pan. Crush the garlic and add, together with the bouquet garni; simmer for 20 minutes.

5 Strain the mixture through a fine sieve and return to a clean pan.

6 Soak the saffron threads in half a cup of hot water and add to the strained fish stock. Bring again to a boil.

7 Lower the larger pieces of fish into the hot stock and after about 10 minutes add the smaller fillets and the shellfish. Continue simmering until all the fish is cooked; do not stir, simply shake the pan from time to time to prevent the fish sticking to the bottom. Adjust the seasoning. Serve this fish stew piping hot with toasted garlic bread sprinkled with Parmesan. Pass the sauce around separately in a bowl or sauceboat.

To prepare the sauce: Place the egg yolks in a fairly large bowl and beat together with the crushed garlic clove; continue stirring briskly in the same direction, adding the oil a few drops at a time. Season with a pinch of salt and a little freshly ground pepper. The sauce can be turned an attractive orange color by adding a little of the saffron-colored fish stock.

Fisherman's risotto

Preparation and cooking time: 45 minutes

Serves 4: 1¾ cups arborio rice ● ½ lb squid ● 1 small
onion ● ¾ cup oil ● 2–3 tablespoons finely chopped
parsley ● 2 pints fish stock (see recipe, p. 175) ●
3 tablespoons tomato paste ● 1 bell pepper ● 1 clove
garlic ● 1 packet saffron ● ⅓ cup cooked peas ● 7 oz
eel ● 12 clams ● 9 oz monkfish ● 8 peeled shrimp ●
salt ● pepper

Suggested wines

Cortese di Gavi, Tocai del Collio, Bordeaux blanc

Suggested menu

▷ Fisherman's risotto
Ham rolls cordon bleu
Cherries à la mode

1 Wash and trim the
assorted fish; cut the squid
into rings.

2 Sauté the squid in the
oil in a heavy-bottomed
pan.

3 Add the finely chopped
onion and sauté gently
until it begins to color.

4 Mix the tomato paste
with half a cup of hot
water and add to the pan;
add the eel (skinned and
cut into pieces), the
monkfish (only the tail is
used) and then the
shrimp.

5 Simmer for a few
minutes and then add the
rice.

6 Stir gently, adding the
hot fish stock a little at a
time, then add the
seeded, trimmed and
diced green pepper, the
peas, clams, saffron
(dissolved in a little stock)
and finely chopped garlic.
Add a little salt and freshly
ground pepper to taste.
Simmer until the rice is
tender but still firm,
stirring frequently.
Sprinkle with the chopped
parsley and serve
immediately.

Jambalaya

Preparation and cooking time: 50 minutes

Serves 4: 1¼ cups long-grain rice ● ¾ lb shrimp, crayfish or scampi ● 1 cup diced ham ● 5 tablespoons oil ● ¼ cup butter ● 1 clove garlic ● ½ onion ● 1 celery stalk ● 4 large ripe tomatoes ● 1 bell pepper ● 1 bay leaf ● 1 clove ● 3 tablespoons tomato paste ● 1 pint stock ● 1 cup dry white wine ● oregano ● salt ● pepper

Suggested wines

Sauvignon del Collio, Chablis, Soave

Suggested menu

▷ Jambalaya
Exotic fruit salad

1 The shrimp or crayfish should be raw and very fresh. Peel them and chop coarsely. (If only cooked shrimp are available, peel and heat only briefly.)

2 Heat the oil in a skillet and cook the chopped shellfish and diced ham over high heat for a few minutes. Remove from heat.

3 Chop the onion finely and sauté in 3 tablespoons butter until tender and transparent.

4 Add the washed and drained rice and cook over low heat for a few minutes, stirring and turning so that it absorbs the flavor of the butter and onion.

5 Stir in the shellfish and ham, together with the finely chopped celery and green pepper, the finely crumbled bay leaf, the clove, the peeled and crushed garlic, a pinch of oregano and the peeled, seeded and coarsely chopped tomatoes.

6 Season with salt and freshly ground pepper and stir for a few minutes. Bring the stock to a boil separately; stir in the tomato paste and pour over the rice. Continue stirring and bring slowly to a boil.

7 Cook over low heat for 15 minutes. A few minutes before the rice is ready, add the white wine, mix well and then stir in the remaining butter. Cover the pan tightly with a lid, turn off the heat and leave to stand for 2 minutes. Heap the rice into a hot serving dish. Serve at once.

Jambalaya is typical of Cajun cooking in Louisiana. Rice is grown in great quantities in that area and the local freshwater shrimp and crayfish are highly prized. The other ingredients may vary, according to what is in season.

Snails à la Bourguignonne

Preparation and cooking time: About 4 hours (more if you are not using canned snails)

Serves 4: 32 large prepared (purged) snails (see method opposite) ● 4 carrots ● 2 medium sized onions ● 4 shallots ● 1 clove garlic ● a bouquet garni (thyme, bay leaf, parsley) ● coarse salt

For the stuffing: 3 tablespoons very fine fresh breadcrumbs ● 1¼ cups softened butter ● 1 tablespoon finely chopped shallot mixed with finely chopped clove garlic ● 2 heaping tablespoons finely chopped parsley ● pinch of mixed spice ● pepper ● salt

Suggested wines

Rosé de Provence, Chiaretto del Garda, Médoc

Suggested menu

Ham, egg and cheese risotto
▷ Snails à la Bourguignonne
Pears Cardinal

172

1 Place the purged snails (see method, below right) in a large cooking pot; cover with cold water and bring to a slow boil: as soon as the snails start to emerge from their shells, turn up the heat and cook at a fast boil for about 9 minutes; drain and rinse well under cold running water.

2 Rinse out the cooking pot and return the snails to it; cover with fresh water and sprinkle them with coarse sea salt, allowing about ¼ oz for every 2 pints of water. Slice the carrots, onions and shallots and add to the salted water, together with the peeled, crushed clove of garlic and the bouquet garni. Bring slowly to a boil and simmer for about 3½ hours.

3 Drain the snails in a colander or sieve and remove each snail from its shell. Cut away the hard, black part at each end of the snail.

4 Wash the shells in warm water and leave to dry on a cloth laid on a cookie sheet. Place in a warm oven with the door open.

5 Work the butter with a fork until it is soft and blend in the very finely chopped shallot, the crushed clove of garlic, the finely chopped parsley, a pinch of salt and freshly ground white pepper. Add a pinch of mixed spice and blend well.

6 Replace the snails in their shells and press the butter mixture into the opening of each shell, smoothing it so that it covers the aperture completely. Sprinkle with fine breadcrumbs and a few drops of melted butter. Place in a hot oven (preheated to 450°F) for 8 minutes.

To clean and prepare snails: Use snails which have been starved for two weeks to a month to purge them of any poisonous plants they may have fed on. Alternatively, if hibernating snails are used place them in a very large bowl of cold water, stirring and shaking them, and scrape away the chalky substance covering the opening of the shells. Rinse the snails and transfer to another bowl; sprinkle with a generous table-spoon of coarse salt, the vinegar and 5 table-spoons flour and cover with plenty of cold water. Leave to stand for 2 hours; drain and place in a clean bowl full of fresh cold water. Repeat this process several times using fresh water each time.

If canned or frozen snails are substituted, simply drain and omit step 1.

Saffron trout

Preparation and cooking time: 1 hour

Serves 4: 4 trout, dressed • 2 packets powdered saffron • ½ onion, finely chopped • a few small pieces of orange or lemon peel • a bouquet garni (thyme, marjoram, a few sprigs parsley and a bay leaf) • 1 cup dry white wine • 5 tablespoons butter • 1 teaspoon flour • salt • pepper

Suggested wines

Soave, Bordeaux blanc, Muscadet

Suggested menu

Mushroom and ham rice timbale
▷ Saffron trout
Chilled peach delight

1 Sauté the finely chopped onion in 2 tablespoons of butter until soft. Mix in the saffron powder.

2 Fry trout for a few minutes, turning once; season.

3 Add the orange or lemon peel and the bouquet garni; pour in the dry white wine. Add just enough water to cover the trout. Distribute 1½ tablespoons butter in flakes over the surface and place in a preheated oven at 350°F to bake for 20 minutes.

4 Take up the fish from the cooking liquid, discard the skin and carefully ease the fillets away from the bones. Strain the cooking liquid. Arrange fillets on a heated plate. Keep warm.

5 Melt 1½ tablespoons of butter in a small saucepan, add a generous teaspoon of flour and stir well. Gradually mix in enough of the hot saffron liquid to give a smooth sauce.

6 Simmer, stirring, for 10 minutes and then pour over the trout fillets.

Basic recipes

Carrot Purée

1¾ lb carrots • water or stock • ½ cup warm milk • 2 tablespoons butter • salt

Scrub or peel 1¾ lb carrots, cut into small pieces and place in a saucepan. Cover with water or stock and cook gently, covered, over moderate heat for 15–20 minutes. Drain the carrots and push through a sieve or blend in the food processor. Place the resulting purée in a saucepan with the warm milk, the butter, and a pinch of salt. Stir well. Cook over low heat, stirring constantly, until the purée is smooth and well blended.

Chestnut purée

1 lb chestnuts • salt • 1 bay leaf • 2 cloves • 1 cup light stock • ¼ cup butter • ½ cup cream

Drop the chestnuts into boiling water and boil for 5–10 minutes. Remove from the water a few at a time and with a sharp knife peel off the outer skin. Simmer in boiling water to loosen the thin inner skins then poach the chestnuts in lightly salted water with a bay leaf and two cloves. When they are cooked (this may take up to an hour) drain; crush coarsely with a potato masher and add the meat stock. Push through a sieve into a saucepan. Heat gently, stirring constantly, to allow excess moisture to evaporate. Add ¼ cup butter, ½ cup cream and stir briskly over gentle heat for another 5 minutes.

Easy hollandaise sauce

1 tablespoon flour • 7 tablespoons milk • generous ½ cup unsalted butter • salt • 2 egg yolks • juice of half a lemon • white pepper

Place 1 tablespoon flour in a small heavy-bottomed saucepan and gradually add 6 tablespoons hot milk, stirring constantly. Once the flour is well blended with the milk, add 1½ tablespoons of unsalted butter and a pinch of salt. Place the saucepan over very low heat and stir constantly until the mixture reaches boiling point. Remove from the heat; beat two egg yolks with two drops of lemon juice and 1 teaspoon of cold milk and stir briskly into the white sauce. Cut the remaining butter into small pieces; return the saucepan to low heat and gradually add the butter, stirring constantly. Make sure each piece has melted and blended into the sauce before adding the next. This will take about 20 minutes. Stir in 1 tablespoon of cold milk, the juice of half a lemon and a little freshly ground white pepper. Keep the sauce warm.

Fish aspic

1 onion • 1 carrot • 1 celery stalk • oil • bouquet garni (parsley, thyme, bay leaf) • ¾ lb fish trimmings (heads, bones, etc.) • water • 5 oz white filleted fish • the white and shell of 1 egg • 3 tablespoons dry white wine • 1 pack gelatine (optional)

Sauté an onion, a carrot and a celery stalk in a little oil in a large saucepan together with a bouquet garni of parsley, thyme and a bay leaf. When the vegetables have softened, add the fish trimmings and water and bring to a boil. Simmer, covered, for 30 minutes. Remove from the heat and strain through a fine sieve. To clarify the liquid,

allow to cool completely and then add the white filleted fish, and the white of an egg and the shell, finely crushed. Beat well with a balloon whisk and heat gently for 10–15 minutes. When the liquid is tepid, add the dry white wine and stir. Strain through a muslin cloth. In order to ensure that the fish aspic sets more rapidly and reliably, you can add a packet of gelatine, dissolved in the fish aspic over gentle heat.

Fish fumet

1½ quarts of water • 1 cup dry white wine • 1½ lb fish trimmings (heads, bones, etc.) • 1 onion • 1 celery stalk • 1 carrot • 1 bay leaf • black peppercorns

Bring the water and wine to a boil in a large saucepan. Add the fish trimmings, sliced onion, the celery stalk, carrot, bay leaf and a few black peppercorns. Simmer gently over moderate heat for 40 minutes; leave to cool and then strain through a fine sieve.

Fish stock

½ lb fish trimmings (head, bones, etc.) • 1 lb assorted fish • 2 quarts water • 1 cup dry white wine • 1 celery stalk • 1 leek • 1 onion • 1 bay leaf • a pinch of thyme • salt

Coarsely chop the fish trimmings and place in a large saucepan with 1 lb of assorted fish. Pour in the water and dry white wine. Bring slowly to boiling point. Add the coarsely chopped celery, the leek, and the peeled and quartered onion, a bay leaf, a pinch of thyme and a little salt. Simmer gently for 40 minutes. Strain.

Mayonnaise

2 eggs • salt • ¾–1 cup best quality olive oil • juice of quarter of a lemon

Separate two eggs and beat the yolks lightly with a fork, seasoning with a little salt. Add to the yolks ¾–1 cup of very good quality olive oil a few drops at a time, beating with a wooden spoon until the mayonnaise thickens. Carefully beat in the juice of quarter of a lemon, adding a few drops at a time. This basic mayonnaise, perhaps the most famous of all cold sauces, can be flavored in many different ways for a wide variety of dishes.

Meat aspic

2 veal shanks • 2 calf's feet • 3½ oz rind of fresh pork • 1 onion • 1 celery stalk • 1 carrot • bouquet garni (parsley, thyme, bay leaf) • salt • 2 quarts water • the whites and shells of 2 eggs

Place all the ingredients, with the exception of the egg whites and shells, in a large saucepan. Bring to a boil over high heat. Turn down the heat and simmer very gently for 2–3 hours, or until the liquid has reduced to half its original volume. Skim off any scum that rises to the top. Strain the stock through a fine sieve. Leave to cool then clarify by adding the whites and crushed shells of two eggs; return to a clean saucepan and heat gently over low heat, stirring with a balloon whisk. When the stock reaches boiling point simmer for 10 minutes. Turn off the heat and leave to cool for 10 minutes before straining through a damp muslin cloth.

Pilaf rice

1 onion • 1 tablespoon oil • ½ cup butter • 1½ cups long-grain rice • salt • pepper • 1 pint stock

Chop a medium-sized onion finely and sauté very gently in an ovenproof casserole dish in the oil and ¼ cup of butter until the onion is soft but not brown. Sprinkle in the rice and stir over high heat for 2 minutes. Season with a little salt and freshly ground pepper. Stir in the hot stock and bring to a boil. Cover the casserole dish and place in a preheated oven at 350°F for 20–25 minutes. Transfer to a heated serving dish, stir in the remaining butter and serve.

Plain boiled rice

2 quarts water • salt • 1 cup long-grain rice

Bring the water to a boil in a large saucepan; add salt then sprinkle in the rice. Boil for 12–15 minutes or until the rice is just tender. Drain and rinse well. Spread the rice on a clean dish towel on a large cookie sheet. Place in the oven, preheated to 350°F, for 10 minutes, for the rice to dry.

Purée of fresh peas

5½ lb fresh peas • salt • parsley • a few lettuce leaves • 2 tablespoons butter

Shell the peas and simmer in lightly salted water with a few whole sprigs of parsley and several lettuce leaves for 8–10 minutes. When the peas are tender, drain and reserve the cooking liquid (discard the parsley sprigs and the lettuce leaves). Sieve into a saucepan and stir in the butter and a few spoonfuls of the reserved cooking liquid. Stir over a gentle heat until the mixture is smooth and thick.

Recipes for suggested accompaniments

Almond ice cream with chocolate rum sauce

Serves 4: ¼ cup sweet almonds, blanched and peeled • 2 bitter almonds • 1–2 egg whites • 3 cups vanilla ice cream • 3 tablespoons sugar • 6 tablespoons light rum • 2 squares bitter chocolate • 1 small piece butter

Pound the almonds with the sugar (or use ground almonds). Gradually work in the beaten egg white (reserving 1 teaspoonful). When the mixture binds to form a kind of dough, press into a fairly thick layer and place it on a buttered cookie sheet; bake in the oven at 350°F for about 20 minutes. Place the dried and browned almond mixture on the counter or working surface and break into very small crumbs with the rolling pin. Combine this with the slightly softened ice cream and place a couple of scoopfuls in each sundae dish. Sprinkle each serving with a tablespoon of rum and grate some chocolate over the top. Serve at once.

Apple and amaretto zabaglione

Serves 4: 5 Golden Delicious apples • 4 eggs, separated • ⅔ cup sugar • ¾ cup cream • ⅓ cup butter • 5 oz amaretti di Saronno or ratafias • a pinch of powdered cinnamon • ¾ cup Marsala • ½ cup Muscadel • a few drops vanilla extract • 2 squares bitter chocolate, grated • 1 tablespoon powdered sugar • 1 tablespoon brandy

Peel, core and slice the apples finely and sauté in ¼ cup butter. Add scant ½ cup sugar, a pinch of cinnamon, a few drops of vanilla extract and cook gently for about 10 minutes before adding the cream. Cook for another 15 minutes and then crumble the amaretti onto the apples; sprinkle with the Muscadel and simmer for another 10 minutes over very low heat. Meanwhile whisk the egg yolks with the remaining sugar until light and frothy in a copper or china bowl, whisk in the Marsala and place the bowl over hot (but not boiling) water; continue beating for 15 minutes; the egg yolks will increase considerably in volume and become very light and fluffy. Remove from the heat and continue beating until the mixture has cooled. Fold in the stiffly beaten egg whites and pour this mixture over the apple and almond biscuit mixture, level the surface with a spatula and place in the freezer for 1 hour. *To prepare the chocolate sauce*: Melt the grated chocolate with the powdered sugar, 1½ tablespoons of butter and the brandy in a double boiler, stirring over a gentle heat until it forms a thick sauce. Spoon or pipe a decorative pattern on top of the chilled zabaglione.

Apple meringue

Serves 4: 2¼ lb firm cooking apples • 1 cup water • 1 cup dry white wine • 1 cup sugar • ⅓ cup raisins, blanched for 5 minutes in boiling water and drained • 5 egg whites • 1¾ cups powdered sugar • pinch of salt • small piece butter • pinch of powdered cinnamon • grated rind of 1 lemon

Peel, core and thinly slice the apples. Make a sugar syrup by boiling the water, sugar and dry white wine together, cooking over a moderate heat until the liquid has reduced to about a quarter of its original volume. Place one third of the sliced apples to cover the bottom of a saucepan, pour the sugar syrup over them and cook slowly until tender but still firm. Transfer the apples to a deep bowl. Cook the remaining apple slices in the same way in two more batches. Reduce the remaining syrup a little and add the raisins, cinnamon and lemon rind; stir and pour over the apple slices. Mix carefully and transfer to a well-buttered ovenproof dish. *To prepare the meringue*: Beat the egg whites until frothy with a pinch of salt and then whisk until stiff; gradually beat in the powdered sugar. Heap the meringue on top of the apples. Bake in the oven at 250°F for 1 hour. Serve hot.

Apples flamed in rum

Serves 4: 4 Golden Delicious apples • 6 tablespoons melted butter • 6 tablespoons redcurrant jelly • 4 ladyfingers • ½ cup water • 1 cup dry white wine • ⅔ cup sugar • 1 cup rum sweetened with 1 teaspoon sugar

Brush a round ovenproof dish with 1½ tablespoons of the melted butter and arrange the peeled and cored whole apples in it. Crumble the ladyfingers, sprinkle them with the remaining melted butter and mix with the redcurrant jelly; fill the hollow core of each apple with this mixture.

Mix the water, wine and sugar together and pour into the dish. Bake in a preheated oven at 425°F for 15 minutes. Take up the apples and arrange in a shallow heated serving dish; allow the juices to reduce until syrupy and then pour over the apples. Gently heat the sweetened rum, pour over the apples and flame.

Apricot and kirsch soufflé

Serves 4: 1½ lb dried apricots • ½ cup sugar • 4 eggs • 6 tablespoons butter, cut into small pieces • ½ cup kirsch • pinch of powdered cloves • 6 *petit-beurre* biscuits • 4 canned apricot halves • 1 cup cream, whipped

Soak the dried apricots in warm water for at least 8 hours. Drain, place in a saucepan with enough water to cover, add the sugar and cook gently until tender. Drain and purée in the blender or food processor. Transfer the purée to a heavy-bottomed saucepan and heat. Beat the egg yolks in a small bowl with the butter, which has been left to soften at room temperature, and stir into the apricot purée. Add a pinch of powdered cloves and the kirsch. Turn off the heat and allow to cool. Beat the egg whites until stiff and fold into the apricot purée; turn into a soufflé dish buttered and coated with finely crushed *petit-beurre* biscuits. Fill the soufflé dish only three-quarters full. Place in a *bain-marie* in a preheated oven at 350°F for 50 minutes. Allow to cool before decorating with whipped cream and apricot halves.

Asparagus and rice mold

Serves 4: 2 cups long-grain rice • 2¼ lb fresh asparagus • 1 stock cube • 1 tablespoon oil • ¼ cup butter • 2 packages processed cheese slices • 6 tablespoons grated Parmesan cheese • 2 hard-boiled egg yolks • salt • pepper

Trim and cook the asparagus until just tender. Remove carefully from the saucepan, reserving the cooking water, cut off the white ends and discard. Cut the asparagus spears into short sections, leaving the tips intact. Transfer the cooking water to a large saucepan, add 1 pint fresh water and the stock cube and bring to a boil. Add the rice, stir and cook for 15–20 minutes until tender. While the rice is cooking, melt the butter in a *bain-marie*; add the asparagus pieces (reserving the tips for later use), season with a little freshly ground pepper and warm through. Drain the rice and place in a bowl. Gradually stir in the asparagus pieces and the butter in which they have been heated; fold in the asparagus tips and the grated Parmesan cheese. Lightly grease a large round casserole and spoon in 5–6 tablespoons rice, pressing down firmly to level the surface. Cover with cheese slices and add more rice, pressing down this layer before covering with more cheese slices. Continue until all the rice and cheese slices are used up, ending with a rice layer. Cover with foil and bake in a very hot oven (500°F) for 7 minutes. Remove the foil, cover the casserole with a plate and invert the mold. Push the hard-boiled egg yolks through a sieve and sprinkle on top.

Baked stuffed tomatoes

Serves 4: 8 ripe but firm even-sized tomatoes • 1 cup fine fresh breadcrumbs • ½ cup fried, coarsely chopped bacon • 2 eggs • oil • 5 tablespoons grated Parmesan cheese • 2 tablespoons butter • ½ onion • ½ sweet red pepper • oregano • salt • pepper

Peel the onion, remove the seeds and pith of the sweet pepper and chop coarsely. Place in a bowl with the chopped bacon and stir in the lightly beaten eggs and a generous pinch of oregano; add the breadcrumbs and blend in together with just enough oil to give a smooth, dense stuffing. Season with salt and freshly ground pepper and mix in 3 tablespoons grated Parmesan cheese. Slice off the tops of the tomatoes, remove the flesh of each tomato and add to the stuffing (discarding the seeds). Sprinkle the insides of the tomatoes with salt and turn upside down for 30 minutes to drain off excess moisture. Fill the tomatoes with the stuffing. Level the top and sprinkle with the remaining Parmesan cheese; top with a small sliver of butter and arrange in a greased ovenproof dish. Bake at 350°F for 40 minutes.

Bananas Martinique

Serves 4: 4 ripe bananas • 6 tablespoons sugar • a few tablespoons all-purpose flour • 1 egg • ¼ cup butter • 1 cup kirsch • nutmeg

Peel the bananas and cut lengthwise in half; sprinkle with half the sugar, coat with flour and dip in the lightly beaten egg before rolling in flour once more. Heat the butter in a large skillet, place the coated bananas in the hot butter and fry until golden brown, turning them once carefully with a spatula. Transfer to a heated serving plate and sprinkle with the remaining sugar and a pinch of grated nutmeg. Heat the kirsch in a small saucepan, pour over the bananas and flame.

Banana almond crunch

Serves 4: 8 ladyfingers • 2 large bananas • ¼ cup melted butter • ½ vanilla pod or a few drops vanilla extract • 2 egg yolks • 1 tablespoon cornstarch • ⅔ cup sugar • 1 pint milk • 2 egg whites • 3 tablespoons Cointreau • butter for greasing • 6 amaretti di Saronno or 1 cup ratafias, crumbled • generous pinch cinnamon

Reserve 3 tablespoons of the milk and bring the rest to a boil with the vanilla pod or a few drops of vanilla extract. Crumble the ladyfingers, peel and slice the bananas thinly, and mash them up with a fork, together with the ladyfingers and the Cointreau. Add the powdered cinnamon and the melted butter (all but 3 tablespoons) and work together. Butter a cake pan and spread the banana mixture in an even layer over the bottom. Beat the egg yolks vigorously with the sugar until light and frothy; stir in the cornstarch and then mix in the remaining 3 tablespoons milk. Whisk in the hot vanilla-flavored milk. Heat gently, stirring constantly, until it thickens, simmering for about 10 minutes. Do not allow to boil. Draw aside from the heat and allow to cool. Beat the egg whites until stiff and fold into the custard mixture. Pour this mixture into the cake pan on top of the bananas. Sprinkle with the melted butter and the crumbled cookies. Bake at 350°F for 40 minutes or until the topping is golden brown.

Beef consommé

Serves 4: 2½ pints homemade meat stock, all fat removed • ½ lb stewing beef • 1 onion • 1 clove garlic • 1 carrot • 1 celery stalk • pinch of thyme • 3 peppercorns • 1 egg white • salt

Trim off any fat from the beef; mince or chop finely and place in a large pot or saucepan. Scrub the carrot, peel the onion and chop them with the celery and garlic and add to the beef. Add a pinch of salt, the thyme, the egg white and the black peppercorns and mix well. Pour in the cold beef stock and bring to a boil, stirring constantly. Turn down the heat, cover and simmer for 1 hour. Strain the consommé through a fine sieve lined with a piece of cheesecloth before serving.

Beef consommé with sherry

Follow the recipe above, stirring in 6 tablespoons medium dry sherry at the end of the cooking time, before straining.

Black olive canapés

Serves 4: A two-day-old baguette of french bread • 7 oz large black olives • 1 clove garlic • 2½ oz anchovy fillets • 3 tablespoons capers (in vinegar) • half a lemon • 3 tablespoons oil • pepper

Cut the baguette into even slices and toast in the oven. Pit the olives and chop finely together with the anchovies and capers. Add a little coarsely ground black pepper; stirring with a wooden spoon, add a few drops lemon juice and then a very little olive oil; continue mixing in the lemon juice and oil, beating vigorously after each addition to give a thick, creamy consistency. Remove the bread slices from the oven and rub them with the cut clove of garlic. Spread with the olive and anchovy paste and serve warm.

Blancmange

Serves 4: ¾ lb blanched and skinned sweet almonds • 1 oz bitter almonds • 1¼ cup powdered sugar • 1¾ cups water • 1 packet powdered gelatine • 1 teaspoon sweet almond oil • 6 tablespoons orange flower water • 4 candied cherries • 16 blanched, skinned whole sweet almonds

Soak the almonds in cold water for 4 minutes. Drain, place on a cookie sheet and dry in a warm oven with the door slightly ajar. Pound the almonds to a smooth paste with a pestle in a mortar, adding the water a little at a time; leave to stand for 1 hour. Transfer to a cheesecloth and squeeze all the moisture into a bowl. Stir in the powdered sugar and heat *au bain marie* until dissolved. Add the gelatine, dissolved in 2 tablespoons hot water, stir well over low heat and add the orange flower water. Strain the almond milk through a piece of muslin and pour into a mold lightly greased with almond oil. Refrigerate for 4 hours. Turn out and decorate with the remaining whole almonds, arranged like the petals of flowers with cherries in their centers.

Bosun's noodles

Serves 4: ¾ lb fresh tagliatelle (egg ribbon noodles) • 1 cup cooked peeled shrimp • ½ lb cooked mussels • ½ cup cooked clams or cockles • ½ cup cream • 1 small onion • 1 clove garlic • 1¼ cups dry white wine • ⅓ cup oil • bouquet garni (parsley, thyme, 1 bay leaf) • 3 tablespoons finely chopped parsley • salt • pepper

Chop the onion finely; peel and crush the garlic. Heat 6 tablespoons oil in a skillet and fry the chopped onion and garlic until transparent. Add the white wine and the bouquet garni, stir and cook for 5 minutes over low heat until the liquid has reduced to a third of its original volume. Add the shrimp, mussels and clams (reserving one or two for garnish); remove and discard the bouquet garni. Add the cream and season. Cook the fresh tagliatelle for a few minutes only in plenty of boiling salted water to which 1 tablespoon of oil has been added. Drain well and return to the saucepan, quickly mixing in the seafood sauce. Turn into a preheated serving dish; sprinkle with the chopped parsley and garnish with the reserved seafood. Serve at once on hot plates.

Brain and herb soup

Serves 4: 14 oz calf's or sheep's brains • 1 tablespoon white wine vinegar • 2 eggs • ½ cup cream • 3 tablespoons butter • 1 tablespoon fresh tarragon leaves, finely chopped • grated rind of half a lemon • 1 tablespoon lemon juice • small celery stalk, finely chopped • 2 shallots, finely chopped • 2¾ pints veal stock • 3 tablespoons grated Parmesan cheese • salt • white pepper

Leave the brains to stand in cold water for 1 hour. Clean well under running water, peeling off all the membrane, small blood vessels and pieces of bone. Poach for 15 minutes in gently boiling water to which 1 tablespoon of white wine vinegar has been added. Drain and purée. Sauté the shallots and celery gently in the butter and once they have started to color, add the purée and season with salt and freshly ground pepper. Add 2–3 tablespoons stock, pour in the cream and simmer over low heat for about 10 minutes. Beat the eggs with the grated lemon rind and juice and add to the soup; stir until it starts to thicken slightly. Stir in the tarragon and transfer to a heated soup tureen, sprinkling in the rest of the Parmesan cheese. Stir this mixture vigorously with a wooden spoon or balloon whisk while pouring in the boiling stock a little at a time.

Caramelized apricots

Serves 4: 12 ripe apricots • ½ cup sugar • ¼–½ cup Grand Marnier • a few drops vanilla extract • 3 tablespoons peach jam or jelly • 1 egg white • 24 almonds • 12 candied or crystallized cherries

Wash and dry the apricots well before slicing in half and removing the pits; place an almond in the hollow of each apricot half, cover the cut surfaces of the apricot with egg white and press the two halves of each fruit together again. Place a shallow flame-proof dish containing just over ⅓ cup sugar over very low heat, add 1 tablespoon of cold water and cook until the sugar syrup has turned a light golden brown. Add the remaining sugar and stir constantly until it has melted; mix in the vanilla or vanilla sugar. Place the apricots in the caramelized sugar and spoon the caramel syrup over them. Take up with a slotted spoon and place in a serving bowl. Add the Grand Marnier, the peach jam or jelly and 5 tablespoons of water to the caramelized syrup in the pan; cook until it has thickened. Pour the syrup over the apricots and decorate with the cherries.

Caramelized pears

Serves 4: 1½ lb pears • 4 oz *petit-beurre* biscuits • ¼ cup butter • 6 tablespoons sugar • a few drops vanilla extract • juice of 1 orange • ½ cup Grand Marnier • ¼ cup milk

Peel and core the pears and slice thinly. Place them in circles in a well buttered round cake pan. Sprinkle with the sugar and then with the very finely crushed biscuits. Dot the surface with the remaining butter and sprinkle with the Grand Marnier mixed with the milk, vanilla extract and orange juice. Cover with foil and place in a preheated oven at 425°F; bake for 15 minutes, remove the foil and cook for a further 10 minutes. Serve hot.

Celery stuffed with salmon mousse

Serves 4: ¾ lb canned salmon • 8 stalks tender white celery • ½ cup Philadelphia cream cheese • ½ cup butter • 3 tablespoons whipped cream • 1 teaspoon finely grated lemon peel • juice of half a lemon • salt • white pepper

Wash and dry the celery stalks and cut into 2½ in lengths. Place the flaked salmon in the food processor together with the cream cheese and the butter (both at room temperature). Process until well blended and turn into a bowl; season with a little salt and freshly ground white pepper and then stir in the whipped cream, grated lemon rind and the lemon juice. Stuff the hollows of the celery stalks with this mixture and arrange on lettuce leaves. Chill for 1 hour in the refrigerator before serving.

Cherries à la mode

Serves 4: 1¼ lb ripe black cherries • ½ cup butter • 3 egg yolks • ½ cup powdered sugar • 1 pint milk • ½ vanilla pod or vanilla extract • 4 individual brioches (or home-made shortcake or pound cake) • 4 egg whites • ⅓ cup cream • 5 tablespoons light rum • ¾ cup cream, whipped • a few sugar crystals • 5 Maraschino cherries

Wash, dry and pit the cherries. Bring the milk, flavored with the vanilla, to a boil. Crumble the brioches into a bowl and pour the boiling milk onto them through a fine sieve. Leave to cool before adding the butter, which should be beaten to a fluffy creamy consistency before-hand. Beat the egg yolks thoroughly with the powdered sugar and add to the brioche mixture; then add the cherries. Stir in the rum and cream; whisk the egg whites until stiff but not dry and fold into the mixture. Butter a rectangular high-sided ovenproof dish and fill with the mixture; smooth the top with a spatula and sprinkle the surface with sugar crystals. Bake in the oven preheated to 400°F for 30 minutes. Remove from the oven, allow to cool completely and then decorate with the whipped cream and the Maraschino cherries.

Cherry charlotte

Serves 4: 1 lb black cherries • 1 cup hot water • small piece lemon zest • powdered cinnamon • 1 pint sweet red wine • 16 ladyfingers • ⅔ cup powdered sugar • 1 teaspoon cornstarch • 2 tablespoons butter • ½ cup cherry brandy • ½ vanilla pod or a few drops vanilla extract • 1 cup cream, whipped

Pit the cherries, reserving half the pits and 5 oz of the cherries. Place the remaining cherries in a saucepan with the hot water, lemon zest and a pinch of cinnamon powder and boil for 20 minutes. Drain the cherries and liquidize in the blender or food processor. While the cherries are cooking, boil the red wine for 15 minutes with the sugar, half a vanilla pod (or a few drops of vanilla

extract), the cherry brandy and the cracked cherry pits. Strain through a fine sieve and combine with the cherry pureé. Melt the butter gently in a large saucepan, remove from the heat and stir in the cornstarch; pour the cherry mixture into the saucepan in a thin stream, stirring well. Return to the heat, add the reserved cherries and continue stirring for 4 minutes. Allow to cool to room temperature. Line a glass bowl with the ladyfingers and pour in the cherry mixture. Place in the freezer for 1½ hours and decorate with whipped cream before serving.

Chicken Madagascar

Serves 8: 8 boned chicken breasts • 6 shallots • 1 small onion • 1 celery stalk • ¼ cup butter • ½ cup cream • 3 tablespoons oil • 5 tablespoons brandy • 3 tablespoons all-purpose flour • 2 tablespoons Madagascar pink peppercorns

Use a very sharp knife to cut each breast almost in half and open out into one large piece. Peel the shallots and onion and chop finely with the celery. Heat the oil and butter in a skillet and sauté the chopped vegetables very gently until they just start to color. Dust the chicken breasts with flour and add to the vegetables, sautéing on both sides until lightly browned. Pour in the brandy, flame, and once the flames have died down, add the pink peppercorns. Stir, add the cream and simmer until the sauce has reduced and thickened a little. Transfer the chicken to heated serving dish, pour the sauce over it, and serve very hot.

Chilled peach and rum mold

Serves 4: 6 eggs • scant 1 cup rum • 3 cups + 3 tablespoons milk • generous 1 cup heavy cream • 1⅔ lb peaches canned in syrup • 1 vanilla pod or a few drops vanilla extract • generous ½ cup sugar • 12 ladyfingers • 6 tablespoons redcurrant jelly • ½ cup cream, whipped • 1 candied cherry

Heat just under ⅔ cup of the syrup from the canned peaches in a small saucepan and boil until it has reduced by half; stir in the redcurrant jelly and set aside. Heat the milk with the vanilla pod or vanilla extract and the sugar and bring slowly to a boil. Beat the eggs in a fairly large bowl and then whisk in the hot milk (remove the vanilla pod if used) in a thin stream. Chop about ⅔ of the peaches very finely and add to the egg and milk mixture; stir in the crumbled ladyfingers and cream. Pour into a pudding bowl and cook in a *bain-marie* for 1 hour at 350°F. Allow to cool then invert onto a plate. Moisten the remaining peaches with a little syrup mixed with the rum. Reserve a few for decoration, dice the rest and arrange around the mold. Pour the redcurrant mixture over the mold and refrigerate for 3 hours. Just before serving, arrange the remaining peach slices on top of the mold; pipe the cream on top and place the cherry in the middle.

Chilled peach delight

Serves 4: 5 ripe peaches • 1 cup water • 1⅓ cups sugar • 4 egg yolks • 1 pint milk • 11 oz ladyfingers • ½ vanilla pod or a few drops vanilla extract • 3 table-spoons redcurrant jelly • ½ cup Maraschino • 6 slices canned peaches • 1 Maraschino cherry

Heat the water and a generous ½ cup sugar in a saucepan and boil until the sugar syrup is thickened. Peel the peaches and remove their pits and add to the sugar syrup. Cook over gentle heat for 5 minutes, turning once, then remove with a slotted spoon and slice evenly. Set aside. Bring the milk slowly to a boil with the piece of vanilla pod or a few drops vanilla extract. (If the vanilla pod is used, simmer for 5 minutes to flavor. Remove and discard the pod.) Beat the egg yolks very well with the remaining sugar in a bowl large enough to contain all the milk; pour the very hot milk in a thin stream into the egg and sugar mixture, beating constantly. Return to the saucepan and stir until the custard thickens. Remove from the heat and allow to cool. Place a layer of ladyfingers in the bottom of a glass dish and sprinkle with 5 tablespoons Maraschino diluted with a little warm water. Spread with a thin layer of redcurrant jelly and cover with a layer of peach slices in syrup. Use half the custard to form the next layer and follow with a layer of ladyfingers; continue layering the ingredients in this order, ending with custard on top. Level off with a spatula and place in the freezer for 30 minutes. Decorate the top with the canned peach slices, arranged to form flower petals around a cherry center.

Chocolate bananas

Serves 4: 4 ripe bananas • 2 egg yolks • 3 tablespoons all-purpose flour • $\frac{1}{2}$ vanilla pod or a few drops vanilla extract • $\frac{3}{4}$ cup sugar • 6 tablespoons unsweetened cocoa • 1 pint milk • 3 tablespoons light rum • $\frac{1}{2}$ cup cream, whipped • 8 candied cherries

Beat the egg yolks with the sugar; stir in the flour and mix in 6 tablespoons of cold milk. Heat the rest of the milk with the vanilla pod or vanilla extract for 5 minutes; when the milk comes to a boil, discard the vanilla pod and pour the boiling milk in a thin stream into the bowl containing the egg yolks, sugar and flour, beating constantly. Stir in the cocoa and return the mixture to the saucepan. Cook over low heat, stirring constantly until the mixture thickens. Simmer over low heat for 10 minutes then add the rum; turn off the heat and leave to stand while preparing the bananas. Peel these and cut lengthwise in half, arrange cut side down on a round dish or plate, radiating outwards from the center, and cover with the chocolate custard. Chill for 3 hours. Decorate with whipped cream and cherries.

Cinnamon pear soufflés

Serves 4: 4 pears • $\frac{1}{3}$ cup sugar • piece of lemon zest • generous pinch powdered cinnamon • 3 tablespoons seedless white raisins • 2 egg whites • 3 tablespoons butter • 3 tablespoons marc (*eau-de-vie*) or brandy • 1 cup cream • 6 tablespoons water

Soak the raisins in lukewarm water for 30 minutes; drain and dry. Peel, core and slice the pears thinly and place in a saucepan with half the butter and all the water. Add the lemon zest and simmer the pears gently until they have turned to a pureé. Remove and discard the lemon zest and blend the pears in a food processor until smooth; then return to the saucepan. Stir in the sugar, cinnamon and the soaked raisins. Cook for a few minutes over fairly high heat, stirring so that the mixture releases excess moisture and thickens slightly. Cool a little and add the marc or brandy. Fold in the stiffly beaten egg whites and divide the mixture between 4 well-buttered individual soufflé or ramekin dishes. Bake in a preheated oven at 350°F for 30 minutes. Serve immediately with the cream.

Coffee flavored ratafia cream

Serves 4: 7 oz ratafias or amaretti di Saronno • 4 eggs • 1 cup sugar • 5 squares unsweetened chocolate • 1 cup heavy cream • $\frac{1}{2}$ cup brandy • butter (for greasing) • $2\frac{1}{2}$ oz *petit-beurre* biscuits, finely crushed • 3 tablespoons instant coffee • $\frac{3}{4}$ cup cream, whipped • a few roasted coffee beans

Grind the almond cookies coarsely. Beat the egg yolks with the sugar until pale and frothy. Fold in the almond cookie crumbs. Grate the chocolate and melt over warm water; stir in the brandy and add to the beaten egg and sugar mixture. Stir well, mix in the cream, then fold into the stiffly beaten egg whites. Grease a mold and sprinkle with the *petit-beurre* biscuits. Turn the soufflé mixture into the mold and cook in a preheated oven at 350°F for 40 minutes. Allow to cool and then turn out onto a serving dish; decorate with whipped cream, sprinkle with the instant coffee powder and a few roasted coffee beans.

Coffee ice cream charlotte

Serves 4: 2 oz very finely ground coffee • 2 pints milk • 4 tablespoons cornstarch • 4 egg yolks • $1\frac{1}{3}$ cups sugar • 3 tablespoons cold milk • generous $\frac{1}{2}$ cup brandy • $1\frac{1}{4}$ cups cream, whipped • 10 ladyfingers • scant 1 cup strong black coffee • 1 tablespoon instant coffee • $\frac{1}{4}$ cup slivered almonds

Bring 1 generous cup milk to a boil; sprinkle in the ground coffee, cover and leave to stand for 1 hour. Place a large coffee filter in a fine sieve and pour the milky coffee through into a jug. Beat the egg yolks with the sugar. Mix the cornstarch with 3 tablespoons cold milk and blend into the egg and sugar mixture; stir in the remaining milk which has been brought to a boil, followed by the milky coffee. Filter through a fine sieve, add scant $\frac{1}{2}$ cup brandy, reserving 5 tablespoons, stir well and heat gently in a double boiler for 15 minutes, stirring constantly. Leave to cool, then whisk in the whipped cream. Mix the black coffee with 5 tablespoons cold water and 5 tablespoons brandy; dip the ladyfingers into this liquid and line a soufflé dish or bowl; pour in the custard mixture, smooth the surface with a spatula and place in the freezer for 1 hour. Just before serving, sprinkle with instant coffee powder and slivered almonds.

Country style pasta

Serves 4: 14 oz *fusilli* (spiral pasta) • $\frac{1}{4}$ cup butter • 3 tablespoons oil • small piece butter • 1 large onion • 5 tablespoons frozen peas • 6 tablespoons pitted black olives • $\frac{1}{2}$ cup dry white wine • 2 packets saffron threads • light stock • 6 tablespoons grated Parmesan cheese • 2 sweet red peppers • salt • pepper

Chop the onion finely and sauté gently in the oil and butter in a heavy-bottomed saucepan or earthenware pot. When the onion starts to color, add the chopped red peppers and sauté for 10 minutes, stirring now and then. Stir in the peas and cook for 5 minutes before adding the uncooked pasta. Stir and turn the pasta so that it is well coated and flavored with the onion and pepper mixture. Proceed as for a risotto: add the white wine first and when this has been absorbed add about a cup of boiling stock – when this liquid has been almost completely absorbed by the pasta, add a little more, stirring frequently. After 15 minutes, add the saffron, dissolved in $\frac{1}{2}$ cup stock, and the olives; season. When the *fusilli* are tender but still firm transfer to a heated serving dish, mix in $\frac{1}{2}$ tablespoon butter and sprinkle with grated Parmesan cheese.

Cream of asparagus soup with chervil and ham

Serves 4: 1 lb fresh asparagus • $\frac{1}{4}$ cup butter • $\frac{1}{4}$ cup flour • 1 pint milk • 1 pint of the water in which the asparagus has cooked • 1 stock cube • $\frac{1}{2}$ cup cream • 3 tablespoons grated Parmesan cheese • 2 egg yolks • generous pinch of chervil leaves, coarsely chopped • $\frac{1}{2}$ cup diced ham • 3 tablespoons melted butter • salt • white pepper

Wash and trim the asparagus and boil for 20–25 minutes in $1\frac{1}{2}$ pints lightly salted water until tender. Drain and cut off the tough lower stems; reserve a few tips and chop the rest of the asparagus finely. Melt the butter in a saucepan, stir in all the flour; add the milk gradually, heated almost to boiling point, and 1 pint of the reserved cooking liquid from the asparagus. Crumble in the stock cube. Simmer gently for 1 minute, stirring constantly, then add the finely chopped asparagus and the Parmesan cheese. Beat the egg yolks and cream together and pour in a thin trickle into the soup, whisking briskly so that the yolks do not curdle. Remove from the heat and sprinkle in the coarsely chopped fresh chervil leaves and a little freshly ground white pepper. Ladle into hot soup bowls, garnishing each with diced ham and the reserved asparagus tips warmed in 3 tablespoons butter.

Cream of leek and potato soup

Serves 4: 1 lb leeks • $\frac{3}{4}$ lb potatoes • 3 pints light stock • 6 tablespoons butter • 5 tablespoons cornstarch • 1 cup cream • 1 egg yolk • 3 tablespoons dry white wine • 5 tablespoons grated Parmesan cheese • 3 tablespoons finely chopped parsley • salt

Trim and wash the leeks thoroughly to get rid of sand or grit. Using only the white parts, slice all but two into thin rings and fry gently for 10 minutes in a heavy-bottomed saucepan or earthenware pot in 3 tablespoons of butter and 3 tablespoons stock. Add the peeled, diced potatoes. Cook, stirring and turning, for a few minutes and then add the boiling stock; boil gently, half covered, for 45 minutes. Remove from the heat and leave to cool; liquidize in the food processor or blender and return to the pan. Mix the cornstarch with 3 tablespoons dry white wine and stir in a few spoonfuls of the puréed vegetables; add this to the pan. Cook over moderate heat for 15 minutes, stirring occasionally. Chop the remaining two leeks finely and sauté in a small saucepan in the remaining butter until pale golden brown and add to the soup. Beat the egg yolk with the grated Parmesan cheese and the cream and trickle into the soup, beating with a balloon whisk; reduce the heat immediately (it must not boil) and cook gently for a couple of minutes, stirring continuously. Ladle into heated soup bowls and sprinkle with a little chopped parsley. Serve with thick slices of French bread lightly fried in butter and a small bowl of freshly grated Parmesan cheese.

Cream of lettuce soup

Serves 4: 6 heads of Boston or bib lettuce • $\frac{1}{4}$ cup butter • 1 white onion • $\frac{1}{2}$ cup freshly grated Parmesan cheese • 5 tablespoons all-purpose flour • $3\frac{1}{4}$ cups milk • 1 cup cream • 1 cup light stock • 2 egg yolks • $\frac{1}{2}$ cup dry white wine • 4 slices bread fried in butter until golden brown • $\frac{1}{2}$ cup diced Fontina cheese • salt • pepper

Discard the outer leaves of the lettuce, using only the tender inner leaves and hearts. Rinse well, dry and tear into rough strips. Chop the onion finely and sauté in the butter until transparent. Add the lettuce leaves and cook over very low heat, stirring until they soften. Season with salt and freshly ground white pepper; stir in the flour and cook for a few minutes. Gradually stir in the milk, followed by the stock, then by the wine. Simmer for another 20 minutes, stirring frequently. Remove from heat, allow to cool, then combine with the cream in a blender. Return to the pot over low heat. Beat the egg yolks with the grated Parmesan cheese in a small bowl and whisk into the warm soup in a trickle. Bring slowly to near boiling point and serve in heated soup bowls, with the bread, toasted or broiled with the diced Fontina cheese on top.

Cream of shrimp soup

Serves 4: 2 cups cooked peeled shrimp • 6 tablespoons cream • $\frac{1}{2}$ cup + 2 tablespoons butter • 5 rounded tablespoons all-purpose flour • 3 pints light chicken or fish stock • $\frac{1}{2}$ cup plain yogurt • 6 tablespoons sieved raw tomatoes • 3 tablespoons brandy • 1 bay leaf • $\frac{1}{4}$ onion • 1 clove garlic • 4 slices wholewheat bread • 3 tablespoons chopped parsley • cayenne pepper

Peel the shrimp (if using raw shrimp, boil for 3 minutes in salted water with a bunch of parsley, thyme and a bay leaf). Reserve a third of the shrimp and chop the rest (shells included) very finely in a food processor. Place this mixture in an earthenware pot or heavy-bottomed saucepan with $\frac{1}{4}$ cup butter, a bay leaf, the onion and the peeled lightly crushed garlic clove. Cook over gentle heat, stirring; add the brandy and simmer until it has evaporated. Remove and discard the garlic and the onion and stir in the flour. Stir until it turns a reddish color and then gradually blend in the stock. When the sauce has thickened, add the sieved tomatoes and simmer for 30 minutes, stirring frequently. Push this mixture through a fine sieve and return the purée to the saucepan. Add the yogurt and cream. Heat to just below boiling point; stir in a pinch of cayenne pepper and add the reserved whole shrimp. Simmer for a few minutes more and then pour into a heated tureen. Sprinkle with finely chopped parsley and serve with the bread lightly fried in the rest of the butter.

Exotic fruit salad

Serves 4: 2 kiwi fruit • 1 grapefruit • 1 avocado • 4 fresh pineapple rings • 6 lychees (canned) • 2 bananas • 1 cup dark rum • juice of 2 lemons • $\frac{1}{2}$ cup sugar • a few drops vanilla extract

Cut the avocado lengthwise in half; remove the pit, peel and dice. Dice the pineapple and mix carefully with the avocado. Slice the bananas into a separate bowl, sprinkle with lemon juice to prevent discoloration and add to the avocado and pineapple. Peel and dice the kiwi fruit, slice the drained lychees and mix with the other fruits. Cut the grapefruit in half, remove the segments from the membrane, mix into the fruit salad and sprinkle in the sugar. Stir well. Pour in the rum and vanilla extract (or chop a very small piece of vanilla pod and sprinkle into the salad); refrigerate for at least 3 hours, stirring from time to time.

Fresh fruit mosaic

Serves 4: 2 large juicy oranges • 2 kiwi fruit • 2 bananas • juice of 1 lemon • 6 tablespoons powdered sugar • a few drops vanilla extract • 8 canned cherries • 8 almonds, lightly browned • 6 tablespoons Cointreau

Peel the oranges, cutting away all the pith, and the kiwi fruit. Slice into rounds and mix together in a shallow dish. Peel the bananas, slice into rounds, mix with half the lemon juice to prevent discoloration and add to the other fruit. Add the well-drained pitted cherries. Sprinkle the mixed fruit with the powdered sugar, the remaining lemon juice and the vanilla extract. Cover and refrigerate for 3 hours. Arrange the fruit in a pattern on a round, fairly shallow plate, working from the outside rim inwards, beginning with the orange slices overlapping one another slightly, then the kiwi fruit slices overlapping the orange slices, and so on. Place the banana slices in the center of the plate and decorate with the cherries, each with a toasted almond stuck into its center. Sprinkle with Cointreau and serve.

Grapes with pink cream

Serves 4: 1 lb white grapes • 6 tablespoons strawberry jelly • 1 cup cream, whipped • 6 tablespoons powdered sugar • $\frac{1}{4}$ cup Maraschino (cherry-flavored liqueur)

Select the plumpest, most attractive grapes, blanch for a couple of seconds in boiling water, peel and remove seeds. Place in a glass bowl and sprinkle with powdered sugar and 6 tablespoons Maraschino. Stir gently so that the grapes absorb the flavors and refrigerate for 3 hours. Shortly before serving, soften the strawberry jelly in a small saucepan over a low heat together with $\frac{1}{3}$ cup water and 1 tablespoon of Maraschino. Stir and then simmer to reduce a little; remove from heat and allow to cool. Fold this mixture into the whipped cream and use this rosy red topping to cover the chilled grapes.

Green risotto with mixed herbs

Serves 4: 1$\frac{1}{4}$ cups arborio or long-grain rice • 1 small onion • 2 tablespoons fresh mixed herbs • 3 tablespoons oil • $\frac{1}{4}$ cup butter • 2 pints stock • 3 tablespoons grated Emmenthal cheese • 1 cup dry white wine • 3 tablespoons cream • salt • pepper

Sauté the finely chopped onion in the oil and 2 tablespoons butter in a heavy-bottomed saucepan or earthenware pot. Wash the herbs, pick the leaves off and blend in the food processor together with the stock and a little salt and freshly ground pepper. When the onions have just started to color, add the rice, stir and cook for a minute or two and then add the dry white wine. Once the wine has been absorbed, add the stock a little at a time until the rice is tender but still firm. Just before turning off the heat, stir in the grated Emmenthal and the cream and add the remaining butter, cut into small pieces. Cover and leave to stand for a minute or two before serving.

Ham and walnut risotto

Serves 4: 1$\frac{3}{4}$ cups arborio or long-grain rice • 2 tablespoons butter • $\frac{1}{2}$ cup coarsely chopped ham • 1 tablespoon oil • 2 shallots • 18 walnuts • $\frac{3}{4}$ cup dry white wine • 1 bay leaf • $\frac{1}{3}$ cup cream • 2 pints hot stock • 5 tablespoons grated Parmesan cheese • salt • white pepper

Melt 1$\frac{1}{2}$ tablespoons butter in a skillet with the oil, add the chopped ham, the bay leaf and the finely chopped shallots. When the shallots have started to color, remove and discard the bay leaf and sprinkle in the rice. Stir the rice for a few minutes, so that the grains are impregnated with the flavors; pour in the dry white wine and when it has been absorbed, begin adding the boiling stock 1 cup at a time, adding more as the rice absorbs the moisture. Coarsely chop 14 of the walnuts and add to the rice; continue cooking for 5 minutes and then pour in the cream. Continue cooking for about 5 minutes more before adding the remaining butter, grated Parmesan cheese, salt and freshly ground pepper. Give the risotto one last stir, turn off the heat, cover and leave to stand for 3 minutes. Heap the risotto into a heated serving dish and garnish with the remaining walnut halves.

Ham rolls cordon bleu

Serves 4: 4 large slices ham, cut in half • 1 teaspoon mustard • $\frac{1}{4}$ lb chicken breast • 1 slice white bread, crusts removed, soaked in milk and squeezed out • 5 tablespoons grated Parmesan cheese • 1 egg • a few tablespoons flour • $\frac{1}{4}$ cup butter • 3 tablespoons milk • 4 cheese slices, cut in half • 2 sage leaves • salt • pepper

Grind the chicken breast twice with the bread to form a paste. Place in a bowl and blend with the egg, grated Parmesan cheese, finely chopped sage leaves and a little salt and freshly ground pepper. Spread one surface of the ham slices with a little mustard and place a spoonful of the stuffing in the center of each slice. Roll up and secure with toothpicks or small steel skewers. Dust lightly with flour and sauté in hot butter for a few minutes, turning once or twice. Sprinkle with 3 tablespoons milk and arrange a slice of cheese on top of each ham roll. Cover and simmer for 5 minutes. Serve very hot.

Hot savory toasts

Serves 4: 8 $\frac{3}{4}$-inch thick slices from a very large brioche or a day-old loaf of bread • 6 tablespoons butter • $\frac{1}{2}$ cup cream • 1 cup grated Gruyère cheese • 3 large red onions • $\frac{1}{2}$ teaspoon cornstarch • a few drops Worcestershire sauce • half a stock cube • 6 tablespoons beer • $\frac{1}{2}$ cup water • salt • pepper

Peel the onions; soak in cold water for 1 hour, drain and slice very finely. Heat 5 tablespoons of butter in a saucepan and add the onions as soon as it has melted. Stir the onions over very low heat until they are tender and transparent. Add a pinch of salt, the crumbled half stock cube, a little freshly ground pepper, the beer, water and a few drops of Worcestershire sauce; stir in the cornstarch and cook for a few minutes. Sprinkle the slices of bread or brioche with the cream, spread each slice with a little onion mixture and top with plenty of grated Gruyère. Season with pepper and top each slice with a couple of slivers of butter. Arrange in a buttered oven-proof dish and place in a hot oven (400°F) for 15 minutes for the topping to brown.

Hot mozzarella hors-d'œuvre

Serves 4: 1 large firm eggplant • 4 eggs • 9 oz mozzarella • 2 tablespoons butter • 3 tablespoons cream • a few spoonfuls of all-purpose flour • 1 cup oil • pinch dried oregano • salt • pepper

Wash and dry the eggplant and cut into round, even slices. Sprinkle with a little salt and place on a plate. Leave to drain for 1 hour and then dry with paper towels. Coat lightly with flour and place a few at a time in a sieve to shake off any excess. Heat the oil in a heavy cast-iron skillet over moderate heat. When the oil is very hot, add the floured eggplant slices and fry until golden brown on both sides. Dice the mozzarella, mix with the beaten eggs, add salt and a little freshly ground pepper and stir in the cream and oregano. Melt the butter in a small saucepan over very gentle heat, pour in the egg and cheese mixture and allow to scramble while stirring. Place the fried eggplant slices in an ovenproof dish, top each one with a generous spoonful of the egg and cheese mixture and place in a preheated oven at 350°F for 5 minutes. Serve very hot.

Iced melon cream

Serves 4: 1 ripe honeydew melon • 1 cup water • 1¼ cups sugar • juice of 2 lemons • 3 tablespoons Cointreau • 1 teaspoon orange flower water • 1 packet gelatine • 3 egg whites • 1¼ cups cream, whipped • 16 small leaves fresh mint

Use a melon scoop to make 4 melon balls from the melon and set aside in the refrigerator. Discard the seeds and scoop the flesh from the rind; liquidize in the food processor. Make a fairly thick sugar syrup by boiling the sugar and water together in a heavy-bottomed saucepan until thick. Blend this syrup with the liquidized melon pulp, the lemon juice, Cointreau and the orange flower water. Dissolve the gelatine in 2 tablespoons hot water, then stir into the melon mixture, making sure it is evenly distributed. Fold in the whipped cream a little at a time. Beat the egg whites until stiff; fold these into the mixture. Spoon into individual parfait glasses. Refrigerate for at least 3 hours. Before serving, place a melon ball, rolled in sugar if you prefer, on top of each dish. Arrange four mint leaves around each melon ball.

Lemon chiffon

Serves 4: 6 eggs, separated • juice of 3 lemons • grated rind of 1 lemon • ⅔ cup sugar • 1 cup water • 1 packet gelatine • 1¼ cups cream, whipped

Beat the egg yolks with the sugar vigorously until they are pale and frothy. Beat in the strained lemon juice, the grated lemon rind and scant 1 cup water. Cook over very low heat or in a double boiler, stirring constantly until the mixture thickens (do not allow to boil). Remove from heat and leave to stand until lukewarm; fold in 1¼ cups whipped cream. Dissolve the gelatine in 2 tablespoons hot water and stir into the lemon cream. Mix gently but thoroughly and fold into the stiffly beaten egg whites. Place in the freezer for 1 hour before serving.

Lettuce and ham risotto

Serves 4: 1¾ cups arborio or long-grain rice • ¼ cup butter • 1 large white onion • 2 heads of lettuce • ½ cup diced ham • ¾ cup dry white wine • 3 tablespoons grated Parmesan cheese • 6 tablespoons cream • 2 pints hot stock • 1 tablespoon chopped parsley • salt • white pepper

Chop the onion finely and fry gently in 2 tablespoons of butter; after a few minutes gradually add 3 tablespoons stock. After about 10 minutes, when the onion should be tender but not browned, add the shredded lettuce. Stir and fry gently until the lettuce has softened. Add the diced ham and cook over slightly higher heat for 5 minutes. Sprinkle the rice into the pan and cook for a minute or two, stirring constantly. Pour in the dry white wine and heat until it is absorbed. Add about 1 cup boiling stock and continue cooking and stirring until the rice has absorbed almost all the liquid, then add about half a cup more; continue adding the stock and stirring until the rice is tender but still firm. Pour in the cream and the grated Parmesan cheese; stir briefly and turn off the heat. Stir in the remaining butter, cut into small pieces, cover and leave to stand for a couple of minutes. Sprinkle with freshly ground pepper and the chopped parsley just before serving.

Melon filled with fruit salad

Serves 4: 1 honeydew melon • 2 ripe apricots • 1 ripe peach • 1 banana • juice of half a lemon • 3 tablespoons seedless white raisins • ¼ cup powdered sugar • a few drops vanilla extract • 1 cup kirsch

Wash, skin and pit the apricots and the peach; dice and place in a large bowl with the raisins; stir in 6 tablespoons of powdered sugar, a few drops of vanilla extract and the kirsch. Peel and slice the banana into rings, sprinkle with lemon juice and the remaining powdered sugar. Slice off the top of the melon, scoop out the flesh and discard the seeds. Dice the melon flesh and add, together with its juice, to the fruit soaking in the kirsch. Refrigerate for 1 hour and then mix in the banana slices; spoon into the hollowed-out melon, replace the top of the melon and chill for a further 3 hours or longer.

Mixed dried fruit in spiced wine and kirsch

Serves 4: 8 prunes • 6 dried apricots • 6 dates • 6 walnuts • 12 slivered almonds • 4 dried figs • 6 tablespoons honey • 1 cup Muscadel • a pinch of powdered cinnamon • a few drops vanilla extract • 1¾ cups kirsch • ¾ cup cream, whipped

Soak the prunes in warm water for a few hours and leave the apricots to soak for at least 8 hours. Drain and cut into small pieces, together with the dates and figs. Place the fruit in a saucepan and pour over the wine; sprinkle with cinnamon and vanilla and add the honey. Cook over low heat for 40 minutes, stirring frequently; add the chopped walnuts and slivered almonds. Cook, stirring, for 10 minutes more, pour in the kirsch and turn off the heat. Allow to cool, spoon into glass dishes and refrigerate for 3 hours. Decorate with whipped cream.

Moist date cake

Serves 4: 10 oz pitted dates • 1 cup all-purpose flour • 2½ oz ground almonds • ½ cup Grand Marnier • 2 eggs, separated • milk as required to moisten the dough • 1 teaspoon baking powder • 1 tablespoon sugar • grated orange rind • small piece butter

Use the butter to grease a cake pan. Arrange the dates in the bottom in concentric circles. Beat the egg yolks with the sugar and the grated orange peel; stir in the flour and the ground almonds. Add enough warm milk to give a fairly stiff dough and then stir in the Grand Marnier, which will give the mixture a cake-batter consistency. Mix the baking powder with 1 tablespoon milk and stir quickly into the mixture. Fold in the stiffly beaten egg whites and turn the mixture into the cake pan. Bake in a preheated oven at 350°F for 40 minutes. Allow to cool at room temperature before turning out.

Mushroom and ham rice timbale

Serves 4: 1¾ cups arborio or long-grain rice • 6 tablespoons butter • 5 tablespoons grated Parmesan cheese • 3 cups button mushrooms • 3 tablespoons oil • 3 shallots • ⅓ cup diced unsmoked bacon • 3 tablespoons port • juice of half a lemon • ¾ cup cream • 1 tablespoon flour • pinch of thyme • salt • pepper

Wash the mushrooms, trim and place in a bowl of cold water, acidulated with the juice of half a lemon to prevent discoloration; drain and dry before slicing thinly. Chop the shallots finely and sauté gently in the oil and 2 tablespoons of butter. When they begin to color, add the mushrooms and cook briskly. Season with a pinch of salt, freshly ground pepper and a pinch of thyme. Add the diced bacon. Pour in the port, simmer for about 15 minutes until it has evaporated and stir in the flour worked with 2 tablespoons butter into a *beurre manié*; mix in the cream. Meanwhile, boil the rice for 15–20 minutes in plenty of salted water. When it is tender but still firm drain, return to the saucepan and mix in the remaining butter and the grated Parmesan cheese. Turn the rice into a timbale mold or bowl rinsed with cold water. Place in a very hot oven (preheated to 500°F) for 10 minutes. Cover the mold or bowl with a round serving dish and invert. Pour the hot creamy mushroom sauce over the rice mold and serve immediately.

Orange cream

Serves 4: 4 juicy oranges • 1 cup powdered sugar • 1 cup water • 3 rounded tablespoons cornstarch • ½ cup milk • 3 eggs separated • 1¼ cups cream, whipped • grated rind of 1 orange • 3 tablespoons brandy • a few drops vanilla extract • 2 slices caramelized or candied oranges

Squeeze the oranges and mix the juice with the powdered sugar and water; bring to a boil. Boil for a few minutes, then stir in the cornstarch mixed with the milk. Simmer, stirring constantly, for about 10 minutes. Remove from the heat and add the vanilla extract, the grated orange peel and the three egg yolks, beaten in one at a time. Stir in the brandy. Allow to cool, then fold in the whipped cream and the egg whites, whisked until stiff. Pour into glasses and refrigerate for two hours. Before serving, decorate each dessert with half a slice of caramelized or candied orange.

Orange frost

Serves 4: 4 large juicy oranges • ⅓ cup water • 4 eggs • ⅓ cup sugar • a few drops vanilla extract • 1 teaspoon cornstarch • ½ cup Grand Marnier • ½ cup cream, whipped • 2 oz slivered toasted almonds

Squeeze the oranges and reserve four of the empty orange halves, pushed back into shape. Beat the egg yolks with the sugar and flavor with a few drops of vanilla extract; pour into a small saucepan or a double boiler. Strain the orange juice and stir into the sugar and egg mixture. Add the cornstarch mixed with the water. Stir over low heat until the mixture thickens, but do not allow it to reach boiling point. Remove from the heat and leave to cool before stirring in the Grand Marnier. Beat the egg

whites until stiff and fold in the orange mixture. Spoon into the empty orange halves (set in glass bowls to keep upright) and put in the freezer for 1 hour. Before serving, pipe whipped cream on top of each orange half and sprinkle with slivered toasted almonds.

Orange semolina cream

Serves 4: ¼ cup fine semolina • juice of 2 oranges, strained • ½ cup sugar • a few drops vanilla extract • 2 egg yolks • 2 tablespoons butter • 2 egg whites • 1 tablespoon finely grated orange peel • 1½ oz seedless white raisins soaked in a mixture of ½ cup rum and 3 tablespoons warm water • ½ cup cream, whipped • 2 orange slices, halved and dipped in sugar

Top up the orange juice with water to yield 1 pint and bring to a gentle boil. Stir in the semolina and cook for 15 minutes. Beat the egg yolks with the sugar and vanilla until smooth and thickened. Pour the semolina mixture into the egg mixture in a thin stream, beating vigorously. Return to the saucepan and cook over fairly high heat, stirring constantly for 10 minutes. Draw aside from the heat, add the white raisins and leave to cool to room temperature. Whisk the egg whites until stiff and fold well into the semolina mixture together with the grated orange peel. Spoon into individual dishes and refrigerate for 3 hours. Decorate each dessert with a swirl of whipped cream and half an orange slice dipped in sugar.

Peach and wine chiffon

Serves 4: 4 petit-suisse cheeses • 4 large peaches • 1 cup peach juice • 2 eggs • 6 tablespoons sugar • a few drops vanilla extract • 3 tablespoons brandy • 1 cup cream, whipped and sweetened

Cover the peaches with boiling water for 2–3 minutes to remove the skins, pit the peaches and slice finely. Place the slices in a bowl and sprinkle with 3 tablespoons of sugar mixed with the vanilla and brandy. Cover and refrigerate for 2 hours. Reserve 4 peach slices and purée the remainder in a blender with the juices and brandy, the petit-suisse cheeses and peach juice. Beat the egg yolks with the remaining sugar until light and frothy, fold carefully into the whipped cream and then fold in the peach purée a spoonful at a time. Beat the egg whites until stiff and fold into the apricot and cream mixture. Spoon into glass dishes and place in the freezer for 1 hour. Decorate each with a peach slice before serving.

Peaches and apricots in citrus syrup

Serves 4: 4 large peaches • 4 apricots • juice of 2 oranges and 1 lemon • ½ cup brandy • ¾ cup almonds • ¾ cup powdered sugar • a pinch of powdered cinnamon • whipped cream

Wash, peel and stone the peaches and apricots, and slice fairly thickly. Place in a glass bowl, sprinkle with the brandy, the orange and lemon juice and the powdered sugar; add the coarsely chopped almonds and the powdered cinnamon and stir. Chill in the refrigerator for 3 hours. Decorate with whipped cream.

Peaches with raspberry sauce

Serves 4: 4 large peaches • 5 tablespoons powdered sugar • a few drops vanilla extract • ½ cup Cointreau or Grand Marnier • ½ lb fresh raspberries • 6 tablespoons raspberry jelly ● 1 packet gelatine ● ½ cup water ● ⅔ cup slivered toasted almonds ● 1¼ cup cream, whipped and sweetened

Blanch the peaches in boiling water for 2 minutes to remove the skins, cut each peach in half and remove the pit. Rinse the raspberries, drain well and dry in paper towels; place in a large fairly shallow dish and sprinkle with 5 tablespoons of powdered sugar and the orange liqueur. Cover and chill in the refrigerator for 1 hour, stirring carefully twice. Place about a teaspoon of the chilled raspberries and some of their liqueur-flavored juice in the hollow of each peach half; turn the peaches upside down, keeping the raspberries and juice in the hollow as much as possible by pressing a metal spatula over them as they are turned over, and arrange in a fairly shallow serving dish. Liquidize the remaining raspberries and juice, the raspberry jelly, vanilla extract and ½ cup water in the food processor, blending into a fairly smooth sauce. Pour this sauce into a saucepan and heat for 5 minutes. Remove from the heat, dissolve the gelatine in 2 tablespoons hot water and add to the saucepan to make a glaze. Mix well, and allow to cool. Use a pastry brush to cover the peaches with the glaze or spoon the glaze over the peaches. Chill for 3 hours. Before serving sprinkle with slivered toasted almonds and top with whipped cream.

Pear and walnut cake

Serves 4: 14 oz ripe pears ● 12 walnuts, chopped ● 2 eggs, separated ● 5 rounded tablespoons flour ● ½ cup sugar ● 1¼ cups milk ● ½ cup cream ● 3 tablespoons brandy ● 2 tablespoons melted butter ● 1 tablespoon butter ● salt

Beat the egg yolks with the melted butter in a bowl and gradually stir in 3 tablespoons sugar, the flour, a pinch of salt and then the milk, cream, and brandy. Beat the egg whites until stiff and fold into the mixture. Butter a square cake pan, line with buttered foil and pour in half the cake mixture. Bake in a preheated oven at 350°F for 12 minutes. Peel, core and slice the pears and mix the chopped walnuts with 1 tablespoon of sugar. Take the cake out of the oven, arrange the pear slices on the partly cooked base and sprinkle with the nut and sugar mixture. Cover with the remaining cake batter and return to the oven for another 30 minutes. Turn the cake out, inverting it onto a serving plate, and sprinkle the surface with the remaining sugar. Serve warm.

Pears, figs and almonds in honey sauce

Serves 4: 3 juicy pears ● 5 large ripe figs ● 5 tablespoons lightly toasted sweet almonds ● 3 tablespoons toasted bitter almonds ● 6 tablespoons thick honey ● 1½ tablespoons butter ● juice of half a lemon ● 1 cup cream, whipped ● generous ½ cup marc or pear brandy

Peel, quarter and core the pears; slice thinly and sprinkle with the lemon juice. Peel the figs and reduce the flesh to a pulp with a fork; stir in the coarsely chopped almonds. Melt the honey with the butter in a small saucepan and mix with the figs. Blend in the marc or pear brandy. Arrange the sliced pears in circles in a shallow bowl or quiche dish and cover with the fig and almond mixture. Chill for 3 hours and decorate with whipped cream just before serving.

Pears Bellevue

Serves 4: 4 large pears ● small piece lemon zest ● 1 cup water ● small piece butter ● 3 tablespoons sugar ● 1 cup powdered sugar ● ½ cup Marsala wine ● 1 pint cream, whipped ● 12 slivered toasted almonds ● 4 egg yolks ● pinch of cinnamon powder

Peel the pears, cut them in half and core. Bring the water to a boil with the sugar, lemon zest, butter and cinnamon; add the pear halves, cover and simmer for 30 minutes. Take up the pears carefully with a slotted spoon, allow to cool and then chill in the refrigerator. In the top of a double boiler beat the egg yolks with the powdered sugar until light and frothy and beat in the Marsala a little at a time. Continue beating vigorously as the zabaglione mixture increases in volume and density. Leave to cool and then fold in the whipped cream. Place the pears on a serving dish, cover them with the zabaglione sauce and sprinkle with the slivered almonds. Serve immediately.

Pears Cardinal

Serves 4: 8 small pears ● 3¼ cups full-bodied red wine ● ⅔ cup sugar ● ½ cup light rum ● a small piece cinnamon ● 5 tablespoons strawberry jam ● small piece orange zest ● 3 tablespoons seedless white raisins

Soak the seedless white raisins in warm water for a few minutes, drain and place in a bowl. Cover with the rum and leave to stand for 1 hour. Meanwhile, peel the pears but leave them whole, without removing the cores. In a large saucepan gently heat the strawberry jam, orange zest, cinnamon and sugar, stirring frequently for 20 minutes. Place all the pears upright in a deep pot; pour in the red wine, cover and simmer for 30 minutes. Transfer carefully to a shallow serving dish and spoon some of the syrup (discarding the piece of cinnamon and orange peel) over the pears to glaze. Drain the raisins, sprinkle over the pears and pour the wine in which the pears have cooked into the serving dish. Chill for 3 hours before serving.

Penne with mushroom and tomato sauce

Serves 4: 14 oz *penne* or large smooth or ribbed macaroni ● ¼ cup butter ● 3 tablespoons oil ● 3 tablespoons dry white wine ● lemon juice ● small bunch parsley, finely chopped ● ½ onion ● 2 shallots ● ½ lb mushrooms ● ¼ lb diced Mortadella sausage ● 3 tablespoons skinned seeded and chopped tomatoes (or tomato paste) ● 1 light stock cube ● 3 tablespoons cream ● 3 tablespoons grated Parmesan cheese ● salt ● pepper

Chop the onion and shallots together finely and sauté gently in a skillet in the oil and 2 tablespoons of butter. Wash the mushrooms, place in a bowl of acidulated water (cold water with lemon juice added). Drain, dry and slice finely; add to the lightly browned onions and fry for 15 minutes over fairly high heat, adding a pinch of salt. Crumble the stock cube into the pan and pour in the dry white wine; as soon as this has evaporated, add the diced Mortadella. Simmer for 10 minutes, then add the tomatoes and season with plenty of freshly ground pepper. Continue cooking until the sauce has reduced and then add the cream, stirring well. Cook the pasta in plenty of salted water until tender and add to the sauce. Stir well; add the remaining butter and turn into a heated serving dish. Sprinkle with the grated Parmesan cheese and the chopped parsley and serve at once.

Penne with radicchio

Serves 4: $\frac{3}{4}$ lb *penne* • 2 medium-sized heads of *radicchio rosso* (small, red and white salad vegetable that can be used in the same way as Belgian endive) • 4 anchovy fillets • 1 clove garlic • a few drops Worcestershire sauce • $1\frac{1}{2}$ cups cream • $\frac{1}{4}$ cup butter • 3 tablespoons oil • 5 tablespoons grated Parmesan cheese • salt • pepper

Wash the heads of *radicchio* without tearing the leaves away from the base; fan out the leaves so that the heads open up, and slice each head right through from top to bottom into quarters or eight portions. Dry on paper towels. Chop the anchovy fillets. Heat the butter and oil over low heat in a heavy-bottomed saucepan and sauté the slightly crushed garlic clove. When the garlic starts to color, remove and discard; add the *radicchio* to the hot oil and butter and after they have sautéed gently for a few minutes sprinkle with salt, freshly ground pepper and a few drops Worcestershire sauce. Take up with a slotted spoon and keep warm. Work the chopped anchovy fillets into the oil and butter; add the cream and stir over a low heat. Return the *radicchio* pieces to the pan, turning so that they can absorb the flavors of the sauce. Cook the *penne* separately in boiling salted water until al dente and add to the *radicchio* sauce. Mix together well and serve at once, topped with Parmesan cheese.

Pineapple rings in rum custard

Serves 4: 4 slices pineapple • $1\frac{1}{2}$ tablespoons butter • 1 cup dry white wine • $\frac{3}{4}$ cup light rum • 2 egg yolks • 6 tablespoons sugar • 1 tablespoon cornstarch • 6 tablespoons cold water • powdered cinnamon • $\frac{3}{4}$ cup cream, whipped • 4 candied cherries

Heat the butter, sugar, white wine and rum together in a saucepan, stirring over moderate heat for 15 minutes. Add the pineapple slices and cook gently for 10 more minutes. Mix the cornstarch with the cold water, then stir in the lightly beaten egg yolks. Remove the pineapple slices with a slotted spoon and place each on a small glass dish. Trickle the wine mixture into the cornstarch stirring constantly. Return this sauce to the heat and stir gently for 10 minutes until the sauce has thickened. Add a pinch of cinnamon. Leave the custard to cool, then pour over each pineapple slice. Chill in the refrigerator for 3 hours. Before serving decorate with whipped cream and candied cherries.

Poached eggs with tarragon sauce Aurore

Serves 4: 8 eggs • 3 tablespoons white wine vinegar • $\frac{1}{3}$ cup plain yogurt • 1 cup mayonnaise (see recipe, p. 175) • 1 tablespoon tomato ketchup • pinch of tarragon • 8 gherkins • 1 lettuce • 3 tablespoons cream • salt • pepper

Bring a large saucepan of water to a gentle boil, add a little salt and the vinegar and reduce the heat until the water is just simmering. Break one fresh egg at a time onto a saucer and slip into the simmering water. Turn the egg around very gently in the water, so the yolk is wrapped in the white as it sets; poach each egg for 3 minutes and then remove carefully with a slotted spoon and place in a large bowl of ice water. Drain the eggs on a clean cloth and trim off any stray bits of egg white. Beat the mayonnaise with the cream, yogurt, tomato ketchup

and the tarragon and season with salt and freshly ground pepper. Cover a serving platter with lettuce leaves, arrange the poached eggs on top and cover each egg with the flavored mayonnaise. Garnish each egg with a slice of gherkin.

Potato and cauliflower gratin

Serves 4: $1\frac{1}{2}$ lb potatoes, boiled and thinly sliced • 1 small cauliflower, boiled and puréed in the food processor • 6 tablespoons grated Parmesan cheese • 3 tablespoons grated Gruyère cheese • $\frac{1}{2}$ cup ham, coarsely chopped • 2 egg yolks • 1 cup cream • $\frac{1}{4}$ cup butter • $\frac{1}{4}$ cup flour • 1 cup milk • grated nutmeg • salt • white pepper

Butter a cake pan. Place the egg yolks in a large bowl and beat with the cream and 1 tablespoon of the grated Parmesan cheese, a pinch of grated nutmeg, salt and pepper. Arrange the sliced potatoes in a spiral, overlapping in the pan. Pour the egg yolk and cream mixture over them. *To prepare the white sauce*: Melt 2 tablespoons of butter, stir in the flour and gradually add the hot milk, stirring constantly. Continue stirring over low heat for 5–10 minutes. Season with salt, pepper and a pinch of grated nutmeg; remove from heat and stir in 5 tablespoons of grated Parmesan cheese. Transfer the sauce to a large bowl and mix well with the cauliflower purée. Sprinkle the chopped ham on top of the potatoes and egg and cream mixture in the pan and then cover with the white sauce. Sprinkle with grated Gruyère cheese and dot with a few flakes of butter. Bake in a hot oven (400°F) for 25 minutes.

Pumpkin soup

Serves 4: A 14 oz pumpkin • 1 stock cube • 1 onion • 2 tablespoons butter • $\frac{1}{4}$ cup flour • 6 tablespoons beer • $\frac{3}{4}$ cup cream • 1 egg yolk • 5 tablespoons grated Gruyère cheese • 5 small firm zucchini • $\frac{1}{3}$ cup oil • 1 tablespoon finely chopped parsley • salt • white pepper

Cut the pumpkin into wedges, remove the seeds and rind and dice the pulp. Bring 2 pints of water to a boil with the stock cube and add the pumpkin; boil for 25 minutes. Allow to cool a little and then liquidize in a blender. Sauté the finely chopped onion in the butter until tender; add the flour and stir until the flour and butter mixture turns a pale golden brown. Stir in the beer and once this mixture is smooth, add the liquidized pumpkin and stock. Simmer until the soup has thickened, stirring occasionally; add a little more hot stock if the soup is too thick. Simmer for a further 15 minutes. Meanwhile, trim and dice the zucchini, sauté in the oil until they are lightly browned, take up with a slotted spoon, drain and sprinkle with salt. Beat the egg yolk with the cream, the grated Gruyère cheese and a little freshly ground white pepper; whisk a couple of tablespoons of the pumpkin mixture into the beaten egg and cream mixture and then pour this into the soup. Ladle into heated soup bowls, sprinkling a few fried zucchini dice and a little chopped parsley into each bowl.

Rainbow salad

Serves 4: 1 yellow sweet pepper • 1 head Batavia endive • 2 tomatoes • 2 fennel • 2 medium-sized carrots • 2 large radishes • $\frac{1}{3}$ cup olive oil • 3 tablespoons white wine vinegar • salt • pepper

Wash and dry the sweet pepper, remove the stalk, seeds and membrane and cut into thin strips about 1½ in long. Wash and dry the endive, tomatoes and fennel, and slice. Scrub or peel the carrots and cut into julienne strips. Arrange the vegetables on a serving platter in concentric circles, placing the carrots in the center and then radiating outwards with the endive and the sweet pepper, the fennel and finally the tomatoes. Cut radishes into flower shapes and place on the edge of the plate. *To prepare the dressing*: Mix the vinegar with a pinch of salt and pepper and then gradually beat in the oil. Serve the dressing separately.

Rice with anchovies and herbs

Serves 4: 1¾ cups long-grain rice • 3 tablespoons butter • 1 teaspoon cornstarch • 1¼ cups cream • 6 anchovy fillets • 1 tablespoon brandy • grated rind of 1 orange • 2 egg yolks • small bunch mixed herbs: fresh chervil, parsley and basil if available • pinch grated nutmeg • salt • white pepper

Chop the anchovy fillets finely and place in a saucepan. Add the herbs and spices, salt and pepper, orange rind, brandy and cream. Heat very gently, stirring until the anchovies have dissolved and completely blended into the cream. Stir in the cornstarch, mixed with 1 teaspoon of softened butter, and continue stirring until the sauce thickens. Remove and discard the bunch of herbs; beat the egg yolks separately. Take the sauce off the heat just before it comes to a boil and stir in the beaten egg yolks. Boil the rice for 12–15 minutes in lightly salted water until tender but still firm; drain and mix with the creamy sauce, adding the remaining butter cut into small pieces. Turn into an ovenproof dish and place in a very hot oven (500°F) for 6 minutes.

Rice with ham, egg and cheese

Serves 4: 1½ cups long-grain rice • ½ onion • 5 oz button mushrooms • ½ cup diced ham • ¼ cup butter • 3 tablespoons dry Marsala • 4 hard-boiled eggs • pinch of marjoram • 1 clove garlic • ½ cup diced Gruyère cheese • 3 tablespoons oil • salt • pepper

Boil the rice in plenty of salted water for 15–20 minutes. Chop the hard-boiled eggs and reserve. Chop the ½ onion with the garlic and sauté in the oil and 2 tablespoons of butter in a skillet. Add the diced ham, cook for a few minutes and then add the washed, dried and thickly sliced mushrooms. Stir and season with a little freshly ground pepper; sprinkle with the Marsala and cook for up to 15 minutes over very low heat until the wine has evaporated. Stir in a pinch of marjoram and the chopped eggs and diced Gruyère cheese. Add the drained cooked rice to this mixture and the remaining butter, cut into small pieces; stir and mix well. Transfer to a heated serving dish and serve at once.

Roast veal with herbs

Serves 4: round roast of veal • 1 teaspoon thyme • 1 teaspoon marjoram • 4 sage leaves • 1 sprig rosemary • ½ teaspoon oregano • 1 teaspoon paprika • generous pinch garlic powder • 1 teaspoon dried sliced onions • 2 bay leaves • 1 teaspoon mustard powder • 5 peppercorns • 3 tablespoons oil • 3 tablespoons butter • a few drops Worcestershire sauce • 3 tablespoons dry white wine • 1 tablespoon vinegar • ½ stock cube, crumbled • salt

For the sauce: reserved cooking juices from the veal • 2 tablespoons butter • 1 shallot • ½ onion • 1 clove garlic • 1 celery stalk • 1 carrot • parsley • 1 cup cream • 3 tablespoons dry white wine • 1 teaspoon cornstarch • ½ cup stock • salt • pepper

Place all the dried herbs in the center of a large double layer of foil; sprinkle the garlic, onion and paprika on top of the herbs. Rub the veal all over with mustard and place on top of the herbs and flavourings; press down gently and turn so that the mixture adheres to the meat and the entire surface is coated. Heat the oil and butter in a large casserole over high heat and brown the veal all over. Turn down the heat and add a few drops of Worcestershire sauce and the vinegar; when this has evaporated, pour in the wine and add the stock cube, salt and peppercorns. Cook until the veal is tender, turning from time to time and moistening with a little water.
To prepare the sauce: Trim and rinse the vegetables; chop finely and sauté in the butter over low heat until tender. Season with salt and freshly ground pepper and stir in the cornstarch. Gradually pour in the dry white wine and the juices from cooking the veal. Add the cream and ½ cup stock. Simmer, stirring constantly until the sauce is well blended and has thickened. Carve the veal into slices and cover with the sauce.

Rosy Pears

Serves 4: 12 ladyfingers • 1 cup Maraschino • 1¼ lb ripe pears • 1 cup water • generous ½ cup sugar • a few drops vanilla extract • 3 tablespoons melted butter • 3 tablespoons ground rice • 1 pint milk • 3 eggs • 7 tablespoons powdered sugar • 1 teaspoon rose water • 3 tablespoons rose hip jelly • small piece butter

Sprinkle the ladyfingers with a mixture of Maraschino and an equal amount of warm water. Arrange them in a single layer in a buttered rectangular ovenproof dish. Make a sugar syrup by combining the water, sugar and vanilla extract, and simmer for 15 minutes until it has thickened. Quarter, peel and core the pears and poach gently in the sugar syrup; leave the pears to cool. Melt the butter in a saucepan and stir in the ground rice; add the warm milk and stir for 6 minutes over low heat. As soon as the mixture begins to boil, remove from the heat and add the egg yolks beaten with the powdered sugar. Add the rose hip jelly and rose water and fold in the stiffly beaten egg whites. Arrange the pears on top of the ladyfingers with their syrup spooned over them. Pour the rose water mixture over the top. Smooth the surface of the mixture and bake in the oven at 350°F for 15 minutes.

Salmon roll

Serves 4: 14 oz canned salmon • 6 petit-suisse cheeses • about ½ cup thick mayonnaise (see recipe, p. 175) • 6 tablespoons all-purpose flour • ¾ cup cream, lightly whipped • 4 eggs, separated • 6 drops Worcestershire sauce • grated rind of 1 lemon • 2 tablespoons fresh basil leaves • 1½ tablespoons butter • salt • white pepper • a few sprigs parsley • 1 lemon

Drain the salmon and flake with a fork. Place in the food processor together with the egg yolks, flour, lightly whipped cream, grated lemon rind, petit-suisse cheese, basil leaves, Worcestershire sauce and a little salt and freshly ground white pepper. Blend until the ingredients have combined to form a smooth thick purée. Turn into a large bowl and fold in the stiffly beaten egg whites.

Grease a rectangular cake pan (measuring 10 in × 7 in) and then line with buttered foil; turn the mixture into the pan and smooth the surface with a spatula dipped in cold water. Cook in a preheated oven at 335°F for 30 minutes. When the surface is pale golden brown and is firm but springy, remove from the oven and invert the pan, turning out onto a damp cloth. Carefully peel off the foil. Leave to cool a little, then spread with the mayonnaise. Roll up very carefully and transfer to a serving platter. Surround with a garnish of lemon slices and sprigs of parsley. Chill in the refrigerator for 2 hours and cut into thick slices before serving.

Savory turkey rolls

Serves 4: 8 slices cooked turkey, taken from the thigh • 6 tablespoons grated Parmesan cheese • 2 egg yolks • 3 tablespoons cream • sprig of rosemary • 1 clove garlic • a few drops Worcestershire sauce • 2 oz chopped Mortadella sausage • 2 shallots • $\frac{1}{4}$ cup butter • a little flour • 3 tablespoons oil • 7 oz button mushrooms • generous $\frac{1}{2}$ cup dry white wine • 4 very ripe sauce tomatoes or canned tomatoes, skinned, seeds removed and crushed with a fork • pinch of grated nutmeg • salt • pepper

Flatten the slices of turkey with a meat mallet. Beat the egg yolks with the grated Parmesan cheese, a few drops Worcestershire sauce, chopped rosemary, crushed clove of garlic and chopped Mortadella; season with a pinch of nutmeg, salt and a little freshly ground pepper. Spread this mixture onto the turkey slices. Roll up each slice, the savory spread inside, and secure with toothpicks or small steel skewers. Coat lightly with flour. Sauté the finely chopped shallots in the butter and oil until pale golden brown; place the turkey rolls in the pan and fry gently until lightly browned. Season with salt and pepper, sprinkle with the dry white wine and continue cooking gently until the wine has evaporated. Take up the turkey rolls and keep warm. Wash and dry the mushrooms, slice finely and sauté in the same pan for about 15 minutes. Add the tomatoes and then stir in the cream. Put the turkey rolls back into the sauce. Cover and simmer for a few minutes more over moderate heat.

Spaghetti with tuna and leek sauce

Serves 4: $\frac{3}{4}$ lb spaghetti • 6 leeks • 1 can tuna • 1 light stock cube • $\frac{1}{4}$ cup butter • $1\frac{1}{2}$ cups milk • 3 tablespoons cream • $\frac{1}{2}$ cup grated Parmesan cheese • salt • pepper

Trim and clean the leeks very thoroughly to remove all sand or grit; use only the white part sliced into thin rings. Sauté gently in the butter in a heavy-bottomed saucepan until lightly colored. Crumble in the stock cube, season with a little freshly ground pepper, and add the milk, simmering over low heat. When the leeks are very soft, add the well drained tuna, the cream and 1 tablespoon of freshly grated Parmesan cheese. While this sauce is simmering cook the spaghetti in plenty of boiling salted water for 10–12 minutes until tender but still firm; drain and add to the saucepan containing the leek sauce. Transfer the spaghetti and sauce to an ovenproof dish, sprinkle with the remaining Parmesan cheese and place in the oven at 400°F for 5–10 minutes to brown.

Special sweet corn soup

Serves 4: 3 cups beef stock or consommé • 1 cup cream • 1 cup milk • 2 tablespoons butter • 3 tablespoons all-purpose flour • 1 small onion • 14 oz canned sweetcorn • 1 cup ricotta cheese • 2 egg yolks • $\frac{1}{2}$ cup diced ham • 5 tablespoons grated Parmesan cheese • nutmeg • salt • white pepper

Sauté the finely chopped onion in the butter until it begins to color; stir in the flour followed by the sieved ricotta cheese. Gradually stir in the hot beef stock. Simmer over low heat, stirring frequently, for 15 minutes. Add the milk, mix well and stir in the drained sweet corn. Cook for 10 minutes more; beat the egg yolks with the grated Parmesan cheese, a pinch of grated nutmeg, a little salt and pepper and the cream; pour this mixture in a thin stream into the sweet corn mixture, beating with a whisk. Add the diced ham and simmer for a few minutes more stirring occasionally. Ladle into heated soup bowls and serve at once.

Tuna and avocado appetizer

Serves 4: 3 avocados • scant cup tuna (in oil) • $\frac{1}{2}$ small container plain yogurt • 5 hard-boiled eggs • juice of 1 lemon • 2 stalks finely diced celery • 3 tablespoons oil • 2 lemons • 4 lettuce leaves • pepper

Wash and dry the avocados; cut in half and remove the stone. Scoop out the flesh from one avocado and enlarge the hollows in the center of the remaining avocado halves. Place the scooped out flesh in a bowl. Brush the surface of the avocado 'cups' with lemon juice to prevent discoloration. Mash the flesh with a fork until smooth and stir in the drained tuna, together with three of the mashed hard-boiled eggs; mix well and season with freshly ground pepper. Add 3 tablespoons oil, the yogurt and the juice of 1 lemon and blend. Add the celery and spoon into the hollows of the avocado halves and chill. Arrange each avocado on a lettuce leaf and decorate with sliced hard-boiled eggs and lemon wedges.

Strawberries with sherry

Serves 4: 1 lb strawberries plus $\frac{1}{2}$ lb wild strawberries (use $1\frac{1}{2}$ lb ordinary strawberries if wild are unavailable) • $\frac{1}{3}$ cup vanilla flavored powdered sugar (or a little vanilla extract to flavor) • $\frac{1}{2}$ cup sweet sherry • $\frac{1}{3}$ cup sugar • $1\frac{1}{4}$ cups cream, whipped

Wash and stem the strawberries, place 1 lb in a fairly large bowl; sprinkle with 5 tablespoons vanilla-flavored powdered sugar and shake the bowl to mix the strawberries with the sugar without damaging them. Sprinkle with the sherry and chill in the refrigerator, covered with plastic wrap, for 5 hours. Crush the wild (or remaining $\frac{1}{2}$ lb) strawberries with a fork, sweeten with the remaining sugar and fold into the whipped cream; cover the chilled strawberries with this mixture and spoon into 4 individual glass dishes.

Strawberry Bavarian cream

Serves 6: 1 lb strawberries • 1 lemon • 2 packets powdered gelatine • 4 egg yolks • 1 cup sugar • 3 tablespoons vegetable oil • $1\frac{1}{2}$ pints milk • 1 pint cream, whipped • small piece vanilla pod or a few drops vanilla extract

Wash, dry and stem the strawberries, sprinkle with lemon juice and 3 tablespoons sugar and leave to stand for half an hour. Beat the egg yolks together with the remaining sugar until they foam. Heat the milk in a saucepan and add the vanilla; when the milk comes to a boil, discard the vanilla pod and pour the milk in a thin stream into the beaten egg yolks and sugar, stirring constantly. Return this mixture to the saucepan and stir over low heat until the custard thickens. Remove from the heat and leave to cool. Dissolve the gelatine in 4 tablespoons of hot water; allow to cool a little. Fold the whipped cream into the custard then add the gelatine, stirring well. Add the sieved strawberries and mix well. Turn into a lightly greased Bavarois mold and refrigerate for 1 hour.

Strawberry meringues with Melba sauce

Serves 4: 1 lb strawberries • 6 tablespoons sugar • a few drops vanilla extract • 14 oz fresh raspberries • 5 large meringues • generous $\frac{1}{2}$ cup Maraschino • $\frac{3}{4}$ cup cream

Wash and stem the strawberries, drain and place in a glass bowl. Sprinkle with 3 tablespoons of sugar and the vanilla extract; stir and turn carefully. Chill in the refrigerator for 3 hours, turning from time to time so that they absorb the sweetness and flavor. Crumble the meringues and add to the strawberries. Wash and drain the raspberries and liquidize in the food processor together with the Maraschino and remaining sugar. Add the cream and blend for a few seconds in the food processor. Pour the sauce onto the strawberries and meringues, mix briefly and serve at once.

Tuna and pickled pepper canapés

Serves 4: 8 slices day-old white bread • $\frac{1}{2}$ cup tuna (in oil) • 1 hard-boiled egg • 2 anchovy fillets • 3 tablespoons pickled red and yellow sweet peppers, cut into thin strips • 2 tablespoons softened butter • 1 tablespoon mayonnaise • $2\frac{1}{2}$ teaspoons mustard • $\frac{1}{2}$ teaspoon chopped capers • 1 tablespoon finely chopped parsley • pinch paprika • 16 black olives

Cut the crusts off the bread and cut each slice in half diagonally. Beat the softened butter with the mayonnaise and mustard. Drain and flake the tuna into the finely chopped hard-boiled egg, anchovy fillets and capers; mix with the peppers and stir in the mayonnaise mixture. Season with paprika and add the chopped parsley. Spread each triangle of bread with the topping and place a pitted black olive in the center of each.

Vegetable and cheese quiche

Serves 4: $2\frac{1}{4}$ cups all-purpose flour • 1 cup butter • $\frac{1}{3}$ cup ice water • $1\frac{3}{4}$ lb fresh zucchini • 5 eggs • scant $\frac{3}{4}$ cup cream • 6 tablespoons grated Gruyère cheese • 1 clove garlic • generous pinch marjoram • salt • pepper

To prepare the pastry: Sift the flour into a large mixing bowl. Cut in $\frac{1}{2}$ cup of butter, softened at room temperature. Rub the butter into the flour until the mixture resembles fine crumbs; form into a heap with a well in the middle. Add a pinch of salt and the ice water; mix in as quickly as possible and shape into a ball. Wrap the dough ball in a damp cloth and put in a cool place (but not in the refrigerator) for 1 hour. Meanwhile wash, trim and finely slice the zucchini. Heat the butter in a skillet, add the peeled garlic clove and the sliced zucchini and fry until the latter are lightly browned. Discard the garlic clove; season with salt and freshly ground pepper; add the marjoram and then remove from the heat. Roll the pastry out into a thin sheet and line a buttered 9 in flan dish. Bake the crust 'blind', using a cupful of dried beans or lentils to prevent the bottom from rising while baking; cook for 10–15 minutes at 400°F. Beat the eggs in a large mixing bowl and blend with the cream, grated Gruyère cheese and a pinch of salt. Pour onto the zucchini. Remove the crust from the oven, carefully tip out the beans and fill with the egg and vegetable mixture. Raise the oven temperature to 450°F. Return the pie to the oven and bake for another 25 minutes. Cover the pastry with foil if it browns too much. Serve very hot, straight from the oven.

Vegetarian "caviar"

Serves 4: 5 large eggplants • $\frac{1}{3}$ cup oil • juice of 2 lemons • 2 cloves garlic • 6 lettuce leaves • 2 firm tomatoes, quartered • 8 large black olives • 2 hard-boiled eggs, quartered • 8 triangles toasted white bread • salt • pepper

Turn on the oven to 475°F for 10 minutes and then place the washed and dried eggplants on a foil-lined baking sheet in the hottest part of the oven. Bake, turning frequently until they are tender. Remove from the oven and cut each one in half; spoon out the soft flesh from each piece very carefully. Blend this pulp in the food processor until smooth and creamy. Remove the skin from the garlic cloves and grind in a small mortar, adding half the oil a little at a time by trickling it down the side of the mortar. Season with a little freshly ground pepper. Add this garlic paste to the eggplant purée, blending very well. Add the rest of the oil in a very thin stream, stirring clockwise with a wooden spoon. Add the strained lemon juice in the same way. Arrange the lettuce leaves around the inside of a fairly deep serving dish and spoon the 'caviar' into a mound in the center; smooth the surface with a spatula rinsed in cold water. Arrange the triangles of toast around the edge and garnish with the black olives and the tomato and egg wedges.

List of Recipes